CORNISH CYCLE RIDES

LIZ HURLEY

MUDLARK'S PRESS

Cornish Cycle Rides

First Edition, 2022

ISBN: 978-1-913628-05-5

Maps by OpenStreetMap

Cover Design: Andy Bridge
Typesetting: Alt 19 Creative
Editor: Melanie Underwood
Proofreading: Anna Gow

Photography by Liz Hurley

Except: Penrose Estate by Robin Drayton; Siblyback Lake by Mick Blakey; Loe Bar by Ian Woolcock; Chough by Erni; Camel Trail by Tony Mills; Crowns Engine Houses by Sandy Gerr.

A CIP catalogue record for this book is available from the British Library.

Mudlark's Press

www.cornishwalks.com

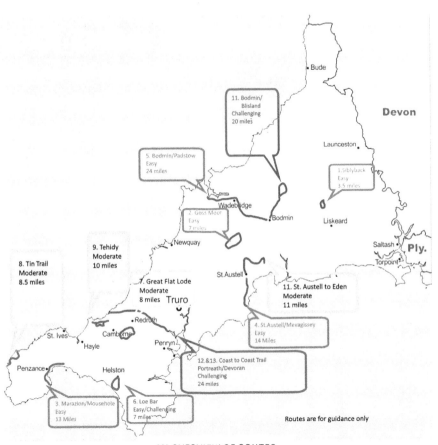

AN OVERVIEW OF ROUTES

CONTENTS

INTRODUCTION

Welcome to Cycling in Cornwall. This is part of the Cornish Walks series but for this book, we're moving a little faster.

I love cycling, have done since I was a little kid. It provided instant freedom as I roamed from village to village. I grew up in Norfolk where the roads are flat and wide and the visibility is excellent with no giant hedges blocking the view. When I moved to Cornwall, I had a bit of a rude awakening. Not only are the roads and lanes here narrow, steep, and offering limited visibility, they are jam-packed with traffic half the year. I stopped riding on the road and went off to find the cross-country cycle routes and I fell in love with cycling all over again.

I am not some sort of performance athlete, even writing that makes me laugh, nor am I particularly fit. Nor am I in my twenties or thirties or even my forties. The point is I'm not some young fit athlete. I just love my bike and want everyone else to have as much fun as I do. I just love cycling, even when I'm mostly pushing the bike!

In this book, I want to share my favourite routes with you. Nearly all have a little bit of road work, but they have cycle lanes or are tiny little roads with virtually no traffic on them. And if you really don't like cycling on the road you can always get off and push.

I have arranged the rides in order of ease and will say if a route is totally traffic free. All the routes offer a great way to explore the Cornish countryside and take in lots of hidden corners and magnificent views along the way. I would also say that if you are confident on a bike then every single route in this book is suitable for you.

If you are one of those fabulous Lycra-clad demons that bomb through the trees at a hundred miles an hour leaping as you go, then have a look at the Cardinham Bike Tracks section. You will love that. But all these routes are also great.

Equally, if you are the sort of rider that would be at home on the Tour de France, I hope you will enjoy these slightly less arduous routes.

Added Extras

In this day and age, a book can only be enhanced by adding links to further information. Each ride features links, as well as a photo gallery of sights from the route, and a GPX download for each ride.

GPX Downloads can be found here.
https://cornishwalks.com/gpx/

WHY YOU SHOULD RIDE A BIKE

Remember when you were ten and the world was your oyster? You got on your bike and the whole world lay ahead of you. You had the freedom to explore, discover new villages, find new shortcuts, paddle in new streams. Screaming through puddles, feet off the pedals, laughing as the mud and water splashed all over you. Bombing downhill faster than Concorde, travelling at the speed of light.

And then you grew up.

You'd huddle in a bus queue for the commute to and from work in the rain. After saving up, you'd buy a car and spend frozen mornings trying to jump-start your beaten-up old jalopy. And the years passed by, and the bills and responsibilities began to pile up.

Boring!

But there is a solution. Get back on your bike. Worried that you might have forgotten how? Trust me, your body hasn't. Worried that you are too big? Well, this fat-bottomed girl gets on her bike every week. Who cares? Cycling is a treat for you. Spoil yourself. Wobble, laugh, explore.

Oh, and exercise is good for you too.

So get back on your bike and have fun!

BASIC BIKE MAINTENANCE

Before you set off here are a few tips to make sure your bike is good to go:

- Check your tyres are nicely pumped up.

- Check your seat is straight and tight. If the saddle is too high, drop it a little, you want to be able to touch the floor on both sides with your feet. Your feet shouldn't be flat to the floor though, it just makes pedalling harder.

- Check that the clips for both wheels didn't work loose during transport; unless you are good at unicycling you'll want both wheels firmly attached to your bike for the whole journey.

- Test front and back brakes.

- Make sure the chain is nicely oiled.

- Pack a pump, a puncture repair kit and a spare inner tube.

- Check your lights are working.

- Make sure your bell works.

Electric Bikes

- Make sure you are fully charged.

- Consider the mileage of the route and plan your usage accordingly.

These checks only take a few minutes and will ensure your bike doesn't let you down.

BASIC YOU MAINTENANCE

Cycling is about fun; pure and simple. You are not trying to prove anything to anyone, you are just out to have a good time. With that in mind:

- Don't attempt a ride that makes you feel uncomfortable or fearful.

- If the hill is too steep, get off and push. I do, all the time.

- Know your fitness levels and stay near them. Exercise is great but the moment it becomes miserable is the moment you stop.

- Take food and water with you. You can't guarantee that the café ahead will be open.

- Take plasters. Just in case.

- Wear a helmet. Always.

- Wear comfortable clothes. Thin layers are best as you can whip these on and off.

- If cycling in poor visibility, wear reflective clothing.

Finally, if you are cycling with others make sure they are equally prepared.

RULES OF THE ROUTE AND ROAD

Even when you aren't on a road, pretend you are. Cycle on the left and slow down on bends when you can't see ahead.

When overtaking, let everyone know you are about to pass them. I use a bell and I shout if they don't seem to have heard me. People are deaf or distracted or just have their headphones in.

If cycling in low light situations (rain, fog, dusk) cycling lights and reflectors are for your protection as much as for other users.

Overtake horses slowly. If the path is narrow let the rider know you are trying to get past; they will pull aside as soon as possible. If approaching a horse on a narrow section get off and push your bike. Horses are huge, enormous softies, and can be terrified of anything. Don't alarm them unnecessarily.

In popular sections, particularly near car parks and steep banks, watch out for dogs, off-lead, suddenly running out at speed.

Walkers have priority over you. If necessary, get off and push.

Obey all on-route instructions regarding road crossings. They are there for your protection.

On roads, never ride more than two abreast, and ride in single file on narrow or busy roads and when riding round bends. This advice from the *Highway Code* can also be applied to cycle trails.

GUIDE TO THE LEGEND

Before heading off on a ride, read the description first. You may discover issues with it. Hills, traffic etc. Then have a look at a map, not just the little one provided with the ride, to get a proper feel for the direction of the journey.

Additional Information: Some rides may be hampered by the tide or weather or may be improved by a few specific suggestions. Details will be given in this section.

Linked Ride: Some of the rides in this book can be linked together for a longer day out.

Length: All distances are approximate but accurate within a half mile. As road and cycle signs are still only in miles that is the measurement used in this book for longer distances. For shorter distances both feet and metres may be used.

Effort: Easy to Challenging. These descriptions are only in relation to each other in this book. Most rides have at least one hill in them and not everyone finds hills easy. Challenging is used for the hardest rides in the book and will be based on effort and duration. However, nothing in here is particularly torturous.

Terrain: Tarmac, hardcore or other. Other is usually a range of surfaces; loose chippings, gravel or compacted earth. In wet weather, these sections can be loose or muddy. Sometimes you will cycle on shared use pavements. This is the only time you are instructed to cycle on the pavement.

Off-road: This is a rough guide to the percentage of the ride that is off-road. Sometimes a section will cycle alongside a road on a dedicated pavement or trail but as you are separate from the traffic, this is off-road.

Parking: Postcode for satnav given. When a specific car park is mentioned be aware, Cornwall is not always kind to satnavs. Have a road map to hand and check you know where you are heading before you set off.

WCs: Due to council cuts, lots of loos are now closed or run by local parishes with seasonal opening hours. If they are an essential part of your ride, check online first. Many are now coin operated.

Café/Pub: Local recommendations, either at the start/end or along the route. Always check ahead, as some will have seasonal opening hours.

OS Map: Always worth carrying the local area map or having the OS app downloaded on your phone.

Nearby Attractions: These are sites worth visiting within a short drive of the route. Some will be seasonal and may have an admission charge.

Map: The map and elevation is for guidance only. It's always a good idea to travel with a full OS map as well as a map app. All these routes are also available as a .gpx file found here. https://cornishwalks.com/gpx/

FINALLY

Things change: Trees fall, posts get broken, signs become obscured, trails can be closed for repair. Do not be alarmed if you can't see a marker. Just backtrack for a bit if you miss a few in a row.

ROUTES

1

SIBLYBACK – EASY – 3.5 MILES

A short, flat and easy circular ride. Perfect for beginners. The Siblyback route follows the circumference of the Siblyback Reservoir. There are lots of places to stop and enjoy the wildlife. On the far side is an impressive dam, which you can walk down to.

Additional Information: Cyclists are asked to ride in an anti-clockwise direction. This is a multi-use path so overtake with care. Walkers and mobility scooters can travel in either direction.

Length: 3.5 miles
Type: Circular
Effort: Easy
Terrain: Hardcore
Off-road: 99%
Parking: Siblyback Lake Activity Centre PL14 6EH
WCs: Siblyback Lake Activity Centre
Café/Pub: Siblyback Lake Activity Centre
OS Map: Explorer 109 or Landranger 201

Nearby Attractions:
- The Cheesewring, a geological set of towering rocks.
- The Hurlers, an ancient stone circle.

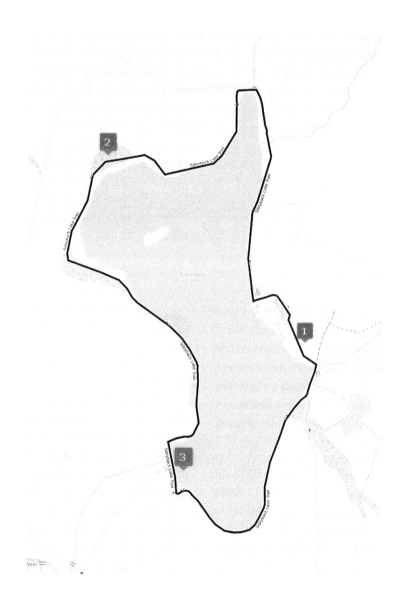

Elevation Profile

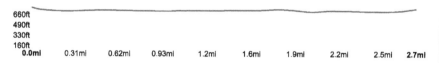

660ft									
490ft									
330ft									
160ft									
0.0mi	0.31mi	0.62mi	0.93mi	1.2mi	1.6mi	1.9mi	2.2mi	2.5mi	**2.7mi**

SIBLYBACK RESEVOIR

DIRECTIONS:

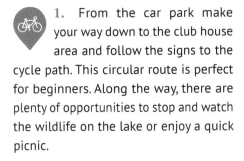

1. From the car park make your way down to the club house area and follow the signs to the cycle path. This circular route is perfect for beginners. Along the way, there are plenty of opportunities to stop and watch the wildlife on the lake or enjoy a quick picnic.

2. There is a lovely section through a small pine wood and then on towards the dam. When you get to the dam, cycle across it and then you can park your bike and walk down to the bottom of the overflow.

3. After the dam it's only a short ride back to the club house. The very last section of the trail is on the site road so be aware of cars.

Siblyback Reservoir: Siblyback Lake was created in the sixties to provide water to the towns and villages below and was completed in 1969. The lake now offers excellent fishing opportunities as well as the chance to kayak or windsurf.

PLENTY OF PLACES TO STOP AND ADMIRE THE VIEW

SMALL WOODED AREA

LINKS:

Siblyback Lake
https://www.swlakestrust.org.uk/
siblyback

PHOTO ALBUM:

https://photos.app.goo.gl/
TqPsNYr8bTMMR14z9

2

GOSS MOOR –
EASY – 7 MILES

A hidden gem in the heart of Cornwall. It is an easy seven miles with virtually no hills and lots of places to jump off and explore the moor itself. You are likely to encounter wild cattle and horses, but they are used to cyclists and walkers and will most likely amble out of your way.

Additional Information: There are lots of opportunities to head off onto the moor, but you will need to push your bikes.

Length: 7 miles
Type: Circular
Effort: Easy
Terrain: Hardcore and road
Off-road: 70% – 2 miles on quiet lanes
Parking: Nr Tregoss PL26 8NE (this is the closest postcode to the car park. You will have to check on the map to get to the actual car park)
WCs: Screech Owl Sanctuary – purchase required/seasonal openings
Café/Pub: Screech Owl Sanctuary
OS Map: Explorer 106 or Landranger 200

Nearby Attractions:

- Roche Rock, a tiny hermitage built at the top of a granite outcrop that the adventurous can climb.
- St Dennis Church, this church and graveyard sit in the middle of an ancient hillfort.
- Castle-an-Dinas, a magnificent Iron Age hillfort.

Three locations that never feature on the tourist trail but are all well worth the visit.

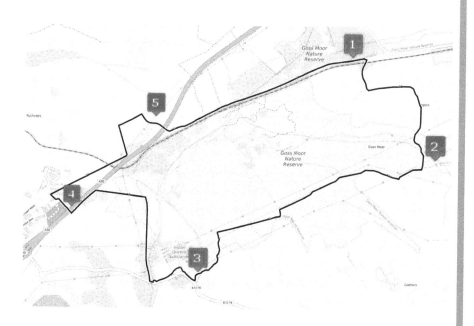

Elevation Profile

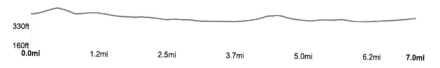

330ft

160ft

| 0.0mi | 1.2mi | 2.5mi | 3.7mi | 5.0mi | 6.2mi | 7.0mi |

THE PATH OCCASIONALLY NARROWS

DIRECTIONS:

1. From the car park, make your way back to the road and turn right. Cycle over the train track and ride for about one mile, pass through a small hamlet then turn right at the T-junction.

This is a small country lane and is narrow in places. There is unlikely to be a lot of traffic but be aware. Beyond the hamlet, the lane becomes even quieter although you are now more likely to encounter horses and cattle. (Distance – 1 mile approx.)

Goss Moor:

Goss Moor is a large nature reserve consisting of peatland and heaths. The entire moor is almost completely flat having been streamed for tin in the 1800s. Tin streaming is a method of creating streams to extract the alluvial metal. No evidence, beyond the flattened land, now remains. As you take the bridge across the new

SHY COWS

A30 you can see how flat the land is. A remarkable sight in Cornwall.

The moor is also where the Fal river rises. As you cycle over the little streams, they are all on the way down to the mighty Carrick Roads that the Fal feeds into.

GOSS MOOR POOLS

2.   At the T-junction turn right, following the *Goss Moor Trail* sign. Cycle a short distance until the road turns sharp left, the trail now turns right, off-road. It is well signposted and there is a small information board near some off-road parking. This first section is a multi-use trail, so be aware of cars. There is also an option to explore the *Marsh Fritillary Trail* on foot. This is just before the metal gate.

Once you get to the metal gate and the cycle pinch point, the trail becomes motor free.

3. After a mile, head through a train tunnel, there's an information board and then the path splits two ways. Take the smaller path to the right-hand side. Shortly, the path splits again. The left-hand path forks into a car park; turn right and continue along the cycle trail. This section of the trail is quite narrow, so watch out for oncoming cyclists.

Just in front of the electrical power station, the path crosses the service road and then continues. For a short section, it runs alongside a road but stay on the trail until the path rises to cross the A30. (Distance from train tunnel to flyover – 2 miles approx.)

Marsh Fritillary Trail: The marsh fritillary is a large butterfly on the at-risk category across Britain and Europe. It is now only found in a few locations on the western side of the country and Goss Moor is one of those sites. It has a wingspan between 40–50 cm and is brightly patterned. Keep your eyes peeled for this exceedingly rare inhabitant.

GREAT FOR ECHOES

4. Cycle across the flyover, be aware of crosswinds. The trail ends at a metal gate and joins a main road. Turn right. You are now heading to the Screech Owl Sanctuary. Follow the brown road signs. The road bends sharp left and then you take a right-hand turn, and then shortly after turn right again until you are alongside the Screech Owl Sanctuary. (Distance from flyover to flyover – 1 mile approx.)

5. Passing the Sanctuary on your right head up over the next A30 flyover, follow the trail down, and cycle forwards. Pass the small car park on your right and continue along the multi-use trail until you get to a gate. After the gate, the track is again motor free. You are now cycling on the *old A30*, follow this trail back to your starting point (Distance – 1.5 miles approx.)

The Old A30:
If you travelled to Cornwall before 2007, the chances are that you were stuck right here in a traffic jam. Incredible to look around and realise that this was once the main road to the west of Cornwall.

ANCIENT AND MODERN LANDSCAPES

LINKS:

Goss Moor
https://www.cornwall.gov.uk/environment/countryside/cycle-routes-and-trails/goss-moor-multi-use-trail/

PHOTO ALBUM:

https://photos.app.goo.gl/4WMEGyAV6PS9ChWVA

3

MARAZION/MOUSEHOLE – EASY – 13 MILES

An absolute winner of a cycle ride. This route runs along the sea the entire way, from the iconic St Michael's Mount to the famous Mousehole harbour. A good, flat path with stunning views the entire way. I love this ride; there are plenty of opportunities to stop for a swim, an ice cream, or even fish and chips in one of the many excellent pubs along the way.

Length: 13 miles
Type: There and back
Effort: Easy
Terrain: Paved. Road
Off-road: 80% – although large sections run on pavements alongside a road
Parking: Marazion Car Park TR17 0DA
WCs: Various
Café/Pub: Various
OS Map: Explorer 102 or Landranger 201

Nearby Attractions:
- St Michael's Mount, National Trust. You will see this iconic tidal island all along the ride. Visit by boat or causeway, depending on the tide.
- Tremenheere Sculpture Gardens has a great restaurant with a few sculptures on the lawns and more in the ticketed section.

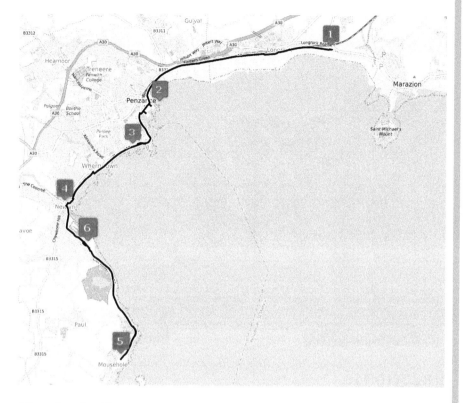

Elevation Profile

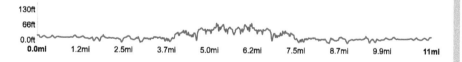

MARAZION HARBOUR

DIRECTIONS:

1. Make your way to the far right of the car park, looking towards the sea and head out on the cycle path. The path runs between the sea and the railway line and you can cycle along racing the trains and the waves.

2. As you pass the train terminal the path becomes narrow and then runs alongside a large car park. Ignore the first right-hand turn into the coach depot but cycle on and turn right at the far end of the wall. The cycle path through the car park is clearly marked; head towards the exit and then turn left onto the main

St Michael's Mount: Approached via a tidal causeway, St Michael's Mount was once home to a Benedictine monastery but then became a stronghold and finally a family home. It was sold to the St Aubyn family in 1659 who still part own it today. The island is run in partnership with the National Trust and can be visited throughout the year.

ST. MICHAEL'S MOUNT

road. This is a busy road but the traffic is generally slow because of the number of vehicles. There is a pavement if you want to get off and push.

3.   Stay on this road until you reach the lido and the zebra crossing. Just after the crossing, you can join the promenade away from the road. Continue along the promenade for the next mile, paying attention to the other users until you get to the far end where it finishes at the bronze statue of a fisherman.

4.   Turn left at the fisherman, and follow the small lane, passing the Tolcarne Inn, over the little bridge and on towards the main road. You are now in *Newlyn*. Join the road and turn left. Stay on the road for half a mile as you pass the Newlyn fish market. The road begins to climb and joins a one-way system. Stay on the road until the houses on the left peter out. Now keep an eye out for a lay-by, just before the 30-mph road sign. The

Because of the tides, you may need to travel by boat when the causeway is submerged.

Newlyn

This is England's busiest and most successful fishing port, in terms of tonnage only beaten by some of the Scottish ports. Like most Cornish ports it was fishing that was the traditional industry, and like the other ports, Newlyn also had an artistic community. Why fishing ports and schools of art went hand in hand is unclear. Cheap rents, good light? Maybe, but the Newlyn School was responsible for some of Britain's finest artists including Walter Langley, Stanhope Forbes, Laura Knight and Henry Scott Tuke.

cycle path now continues off-road all the way to *Mousehole*. The path is shared use, travelling along a wide pavement as you approach Mousehole. At one point you will pass the memorial garden for the *Penlee Lifeboat Disaster*.

5.   There is a large car park at the top of the village, and it might be a good idea to lock your bikes up here and walk down into Mousehole to explore.

6.   Head home retracing your route but remember there will be a small change as you pass through the Newlyn one-way system. It is a short section and well signposted.

TRIBUTE TO THE FISHERMEN OF NEWLYN

i Mousehole – Stargazy Pie and Tom Bowcock's Eve

Tradition has it that the villagers of Mousehole were once at risk of starvation. None of the fishing boats could get out of the harbour during a dreadful storm that had been raging for weeks. Christmas was almost upon them and they were famished. One fisherman called Tom Bowcock decided to brave the storm and catch anything he could, bringing it home to feed the community. They used every scrap he came back with and turned it into a pie with the pilchard tails and heads poking out of the crust and looking up at the stars. Now on the twenty-third of December every year in Mousehole they celebrate Tom Bowcock's Eve and serve free slices of Stargazy Pie. The entire village is illuminated with candlelight and it makes for a very merry evening. There's also a beautiful children's picture book about the story, called *The Mousehole Cat* that has probably been read by every single child in Cornwall.

LUNCH ON THE GO

LINKS:

https://rnli.org/about-us/our-history/
timeline/1981-penlee-lifeboat-disaster
St Michael's Mount
https://www.stmichaelsmount.co.uk/
The Mousehole Cat
https://amzn.to/3a49XHm

PHOTO ALBUM:

https://photos.app.goo.gl/
p76RVhRDRyLQWgbaA

 Penlee Lifeboat Disaster

In 1981 the cargo vessel *MV Union Star* found itself in trouble during a violent storm; its engines had failed, and it was drifting. A Royal Navy Sea King helicopter was dispatched to winch the crew off, but the winds were gusting at 100 mph, hurricane force 12 on the Beaufort scale. As the waves were also sixty-foot high, the rescue was cancelled as the conditions were too violent.

The crew of the *RNLB Solomon Browne* set out to rescue the crew, despite the dreadful conditions they managed to get four people off the *Union Star*. This was the last update the *Solomon Browne* gave. The lives of all eight crew and family on the *Union Star* and all eight of the lifeboat men were lost.

The RNLI is a charity and mostly staffed by volunteers. Whenever you see a charity box drop in whatever you can spare.

4

CLAYS TO COAST 1. MEVAGISSEY/ST AUSTELL – EASY – 14 MILES

Starting at the historic fishing village of Mevagissey, much of this ride is off-road, following the Pentewan Valley. It is a popular route as it runs alongside the Heligan Estate and the St Austell river. The route ends at the market town of St Austell. From here either cycle back to Mevagissey or onwards to the Eden Project.

Linked Ride: This is one half of the Clays to Coast route, see Ride 10.

Length: 14 miles
Type: There and back
Effort: Easy, although one massive hill
Terrain: Mixed. A mile on road, some sections on a path along-side the road
Off-road: 90%
Parking: Willow Car Park, Mevagissey PL26 6SB. Priory Road Car Park, St Austell PL25 5AB
WCs: Mevagissey. St Austell
Café/Pub: Trevithick and Trays Farm Shop & Café, Kingswood
OS Map: Explorer 105 & 107 or Landranger 204

Nearby Attractions:
- The Lost Gardens of Heligan, the nation's favourite garden.
- St Austell Brewery, open to visitors.
- Charlestown, a picturesque working Georgian harbour.

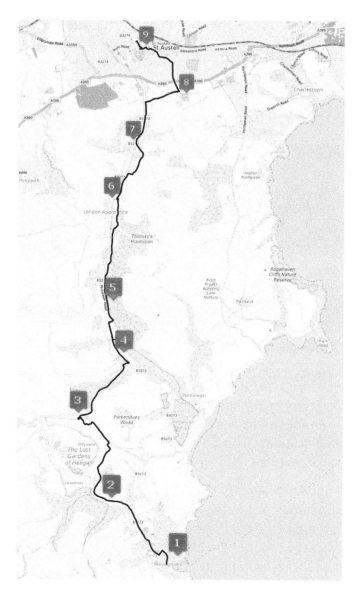

Elevation Profile

260ft											
200ft											
130ft											
66ft											

0.0mi   1.2mi   2.5mi   3.7mi   5.0mi   6.2mi   7.5mi   8.7mi   9.9mi   11mi   12mi **13mi**

MEVAGISSEY HARBOUR

DIRECTIONS:

Mevagissey to St Austell
We will follow National Cycle Route 3 to St Austell and it is well signposted at all junctions

1. Head out of Mevagissey on the main St Austell road. Just as the road begins to climb, take the cycle path on the left. It runs in front of the Mevagissey Activity Centre and is clearly signposted up to Heligan. When the path forks, take the right-hand fork following the blue Route 3 signs. There is a steep hill ahead, be aware of cyclists coming down at speed.

Fishing Industry:
Pilchard fishing was the main industry of St Austell Bay. For reasons that are unclear, pilchards began to turn up in our waters in vast numbers. The whole of St Austell Bay benefited from this bounty, but it was Mevagissey that was pre-eminent in the fishing industry. Although not particularly popular in Britain, the pilchard was highly sought

2.   At the top of the hill is a nice bench to sit and enjoy the views, or just die. Continue along the path until you reach a left-hand turn over a wooden footbridge. The next section has some narrow points and sharp bends so be aware of oncoming cyclists.

3.   Continue until you reach a T-junction.

(Detour – turn left to visit The Lost Gardens of Heligan).

Turn right passing under a road bridge. There is now a lovely long hill down to the valley floor. At the bottom follow the path until it comes onto a small shared-use pavement.

4.   Cross over at the traffic island, turn left and stay on the pavement. Just after the bus stop, turn right and take the bridge over the river.

(Detour – after the bridge, turn right for Pentewan, a pretty beach village and defunct harbour).

5.   Having turned left, cycle along the river. As you pass the first car park make sure you take the path that runs alongside the river. The path then heads into the woods and soon joins a multi-use section of road. There is a car park up to your right; turn left and head onto the third car park. This is a shared-use road so be aware of horses and cars. At the car park, the cycle path continues ahead, ignore

after on the continent. At one point in the early 1900s, the St Austell Bay area exported around 75 million pilchards. To process the fish, they were first salted in brine tanks and then packaged in wooden casks. The casks had holes in the bottom, and a lid was placed on top to which weights were added in order to squeeze the oil from the fish. To further leverage the squeeze, a long pole was slotted into a hole in the wall, and weights were tied to the end of it. The pole rested on top of the lid and pressed the pilchards. The lids were then fitted, and the barrels were shipped out.

Mevagissey:
The earliest evidence we have for the harbour is around 1550 when a stone quay was built in the general location of the existing East Quay, jutting out from the harbour master's office towards West Quay. West Quay is on the other side of the harbour and houses the icehouse and fish

PENTEWAN CYCLE TRAIL

the left- and right-hand roads.

6. Follow the path until you get to some stables, cross the small lane and go through a wooden gate. The river is again on your left. Continue until you get to another gate. Head through and turn left along the service road.

7. As the road joins the main road, turn right. The cycle path now continues along the pavement. Turn right at a white bungalow opposite the St Austell sign. This is a small road but does have some traffic.

8. At the T-junction, turn left and head up to the traffic lights. Cross over and continue uphill. At the top, follow the road as it turns left, paying attention to the blue

stores. The beach and slipway in front of where you are currently standing is known as Old Sand and is clearly where the fishing village began, the rocks behind, providing a level of protection that was then reinforced by the mediaeval harbour wall. This section of the harbour is known as Island Quay, and you can see in old paintings that these buildings were once accessed via a bridge. Across the harbour, the beach to the left of West Quay is known as Sandy Beach. Like all the beaches around the harbour, it is submerged at high tide.

The year 1774 marked the first meeting of the Mevagissey Harbour Trust and was held in the Ship Inn. The Harbour Trust is a charity that exists to protect and promote all users and uses of the harbour; tourists, sailors, traders and fishermen all have an equal footing. During this period, the eastern harbour wall was strengthened, and West Quay (where the fish store now sits) was built along with the jetty

Route 3 signs, ignore the right-hand bend and cycle along Eastbourne Road until you get to another set of traffic lights. Cross over at the lights and follow the cycle path towards the church. Park up and enjoy St Austell and then retrace your steps.

9.   If you are continuing to Eden, keep the church on your right then turn left and head up North Hill and follow the instructions in Ride 10.

St Austell to Mevagissey
We will follow Cycle Network Route 3 to Mevagissey and it is well signposted at all junctions

1.   From the priory car park head into town and turn left along the pedestrianised high street towards the church. Keep the church on your left-hand side. As you pass the church, cycle up a small cul-de-sac with the red brick NatWest building on your left, and head up to the traffic lights.

2.   Cross the road at the lights and take the road opposite. Cycle along Eastbourne Road following the Route 3 signs. At the junction with Albert Road, head straight on, then follow the road downhill towards the next set of traffic lights. Cross the A390 and head downhill taking the first right at the bottom of the hill. This is small and easy to miss at speed.

3.   At the T-junction at the end of the lane, turn left and join the cycle path.

and wharves running along the front of the harbour. East and West Quays enclosed the inner harbour and in a relatively short period, Mevagissey was recognised for the port that it had become and viewed as an important location for coastal trade by Parliament. In 1895, Middle Wharf was built up to connect the jetty to West Wharf. Before this, the sea came right up to the buildings' walls. Reaching out beyond the harbour master's office, North Pier was completed in 1897 and along with Victoria Pier created the outer harbour known as The Pool.

Do not join the road. Cycle along the pavement, ignoring the first turning to Tregorrick and take the second turning left signed Manoa Valley. At the end of this small lane, the cycle path heads off on the right past a wooden five-bar gate.

4.   At the next junction, turn left and then immediately right, ignoring the sign up to Polgreen Farm. The path crosses through a car park and heads into the wood. This is a multi-use road so watch out for horses and cars, the trail through the King's Wood is very popular. Just before you get to the second car park, turn right following the trail signs. After a short while, the trail runs alongside the *St Austell River*. Continue past the third car park until you get to a small wooden bridge over the river.

5.   Cross the wooden bridge and cycle down to the road. At the junction, turn left along the footpath and cycle until you get to the traffic island. Cross the road and then continue left along the cycle path. The path naturally turns right and heads into the Tremayne Estate.

6.   The path now starts to rise up a long hill. Just think how lovely it will be when you return. At the top, pass underneath the road bridge and then turn left.

(Detour – continuing along the cycle path at this junction takes you to The Lost Gardens of Heligan, just a few hundred yards away).

St Austell River or White River:

The valley floor of this river was used for tin streaming, a way to catch tin deposits floating downstream. In more recent centuries the river changed colour from red to white. As China Clay was extensively mined in the St Austell region, the whole area, including the rivers, turned white as they carried the runoff. In heavy rain, the sea itself would turn white where a river ran into it. Even today, in very heavy rain the river will turn a milky colour.

AFTER HEAVY RAIN THIS RIVER RUNS WHITE

OVERLOOKING THE HELIGAN ESTATE

Having turned left we head towards Mevagissey. This section is narrow and has lots of turns, so be aware of cyclists coming towards you, as well as walkers and large family groups.

7. Cross a little wooden footbridge, turn right and head downhill. After a while, the path becomes very steep and on a bend. Stick to one side, maintain your speed, keep your brakes on and watch out for dogs, cyclists and large groups coming up the hill. Due to the bend, your visibility is restricted and you will be travelling at speed.

8. The path levels out as you head towards Mevagissey. As you pass the Mevagissey Activity Centre the path joins the road. Cycle into the village. There are cycle racks by the King's Arms. Bikes must not be ridden on the harbour itself.

Enjoy a paddle and a pasty and head home retracing your steps.

LINKS:

The Lost Gardens of Heligan
http://heligan.com/the-story/introduction/
Mevagissey Museum
https://www.mevagisseymuseum.com/

PHOTO ALBUM:

https://photos.app.goo.gl/xt2SDSTmGrzoGb5i9

5
....

CAMEL TRAIL 1. BODMIN/PADSTOW – EASY – 24 MILES

Possibly Cornwall's most popular cycle route. It is a mostly flat and wide route with glorious views, taking in the very popular towns of Padstow and Wadebridge. This is also something of a treat for foodies. There are great cafés, pubs, and even a vineyard along the route and Padstow is awash with great places to eat and drink, from fabulous pots of cockles, all the way up to Michelin starred restaurants.

Additional Information: In the height of summer the Wadebridge to Padstow section can become crowded.

Linked Ride: This is one half of the Camel Trail, see Ride 11.

Length: 24 miles (Roughly 6 miles between each location. Bodmin/ Wadebridge/Padstow)
Type: There and back
Effort: Easy
Terrain: Hardcore and road
Off-road: 90%
Parking: Scarletts Well Car Park, Bodmin PL31 2RS
WCs: Bodmin/Wadebridge/Padstow
Café/Pub: Plenty, but I like stopping for a glass of wine at the Camel Valley Vineyard about 3 miles out from Bodmin
OS Map: Explorer 106 & 109 or Landranger 200

Nearby Attractions:
- Bodmin Jail, rumoured to be haunted.
- Lanhydrock House (Cornwall's flagship National Trust property).

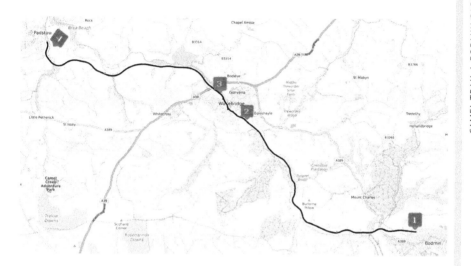

Elevation Profile

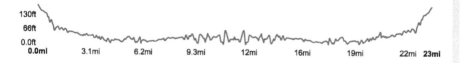

CAR FREE ROUTE

DIRECTIONS:

From the car park take the clearly marked cycle trail heading towards Wadebridge. This six-mile section crosses two tiny lanes and is otherwise traffic free. The route is shaded by trees and runs alongside a river. It follows the path of the old Bodmin and Wadebridge Railway line, and along the way, you will pass old platforms and railway stops.

Bodmin and Wadebridge Railway Line:

This line was opened in 1834 and closed in 1983. It was built to link the quay at Wadebridge and the quarries at Wenfordbridge, to the important trading hub at

As the cycle trail approaches Wadebridge, the trail joins the road; follow this road into the town. After the first section of parked cars, the road has a marked cycle lane. Stick to this lane through the town and out the other side. Turn right at the first roundabout and straight over at the second. As you approach Lidl, the cycle trail continues to the right of the road. It can be a busy

Bodmin. Minerals and sand were imported inland to try and improve the agricultural land as well as offering transportation to passengers. Despite being the first steam-powered railway line in Cornwall, it never made much money. Passenger numbers

LOOKING ACROSS THE STUNNING CAMEL ESTUARY

junction and it may be easier to get off your bike to cross the road. There are several cycle hire centres here as well as cafés and toilets.

For the next six miles, the path is entirely off-road and follows the River Camel as it flows out to the sea. This section is much more exposed than the Bodmin section and can be windy. However, the views are spectacular. As

declined and it eventually only shipped minerals. When that was no longer commercially viable, the line closed.

A small section of the line still runs today, and you may be lucky enough to see a steam train arrive at Boscarne Junction that sits alongside the trail.

STOPPING OFF AT THE VINEYARD

you arrive in Padstow you will find hundreds of racks to park your bikes, whilst you go and explore the town.

The return leg is a simple matter of retracing your route home.

Padstow:

Whilst Padstow originally grew as a fishing village, and it does still have a fishing industry, it is now better known as a tourist attraction and food destination due to Rick Stein's fish restaurant. From opening this in 1975 his reputation and restaurants grew; he published books and became a well-known TV personality. This connection has earned Padstow the nickname of PadStein. Since then the town and surrounding coast have become known for offering the best dining in Cornwall and gradually this effect has rippled out all over Cornwall. I recommend you try the fish dish.

LINKS:

Bodmin Railway
https://bodminrailway.co.uk/
The Camel Estuary
https://www.cornwall-aonb.gov.uk/camelestuary

PHOTO ALBUM:

https://photos.app.goo.gl/3tBzmyQETkuAFfgk8

6
....

LOE BAR – EASY/ CHALLENGING – 7 MILES

A glorious ride around Cornwall's largest body of fresh water, then crossing the beach at Loe Bar. This is a cycle ride of two halves. The west side of the lake is a mostly flat, wide, well-laid path. It is popular with families, dog walkers and scooters as well as other cyclists. The east side is a different beast; the path is often unmade and hilly, running through trees and fields. I love this path as it's so quiet, but it is also more challenging. The views are worth the effort though.

Additional Information: There is no opportunity to swim anywhere here. The lake can suffer from blue algae and the beach has a dangerous undertow which has resulted in several drownings.

In winter or after heavy rain the eastern half may be impassable due to flooding. In this case, simply cycle the west side to the sea and back.

Length: 7 miles
Type: Circular
Effort: Easy/Challenging
Terrain: Hardcore, sand, grass, earth
Off-road: 98%
Parking: Fairground Car Park. Helston TR13 8SG
WCs: The Stables. Part of the National Trust Penrose Estate
Café/Pub: The Stables
OS Map: Explorer 103 or Landranger 203

Nearby Attractions:
- Flambards. Family-friendly theme park with rides and exhibits.
- Cornish Seal Sanctuary. Visit the centre to see the resident marine animals as well as those being prepared for release after rehabilitation, the best way to see these wild animals up close.
- The Lizard, Britain's most southerly point. A much better experience than the sadly commercialised Land's End.

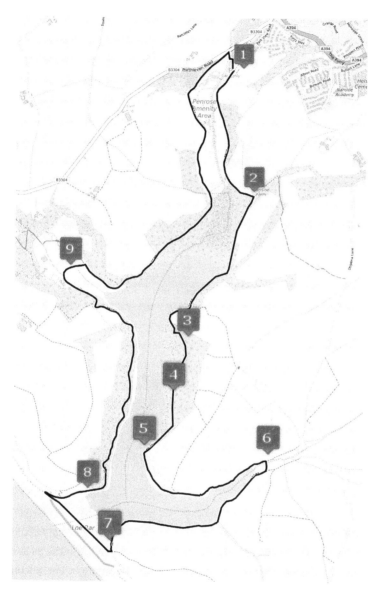

Elevation Profile

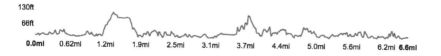

PUSHING YOUR BIKE ACROSS THE LOE BAR

DIRECTIONS:

1. Make your way to the concrete road behind the car park and turn right. The car park is on your right and the waterworks on your left as you cycle away from town. After half a mile as the road veers sharp left, turn right onto the cycle path.

The route is signposted along the way with blue arrows on the posts indicating the bridleway. As ever follow the blue arrows whenever you see them. In summer they may be hidden in the undergrowth.

2. The path opens onto pastureland, which can be wet and muddy. Stick to the left and follow the trail through the field and into the trees. As the trail opens

The Loe:

The Loe was once the estuary of the River Cober but with the emergence of the shingle bar, the estuary became a lake. This can cause flooding issues in the nearby town of Helston as the river has no means of rapid dispersal in heavy rains. In the past, the Loe Bar would be cut, allowing a channel for the lake to empty onto the beach and down to the sea. New pumps have now been installed on the beach, into a triangular clearing, take the route in the middle. After a while, it will re-join the lower path. There are two main paths in these woods one for walkers and one for bikes. The cycle path is always the higher of the two.

3.　You now need to take the sharp left-hand path that heads straight uphill. The trail is steep and covered in tree roots. Pushing your bike seems a good call. As the path flattens out and bears right you pass a large tree. I'm afraid you then need to head uphill again taking the path to the left.

4.　At the top follow the path, taking the right-hand fork as it veers right and travels through the top of the woods. At the next fork, take the right-hand path

removing water from the lake to mitigate the need for another cut.

AWAY FROM THE CROWDS

CROSSING THE CARMINOWE CREEK

and head downhill back towards the *Loe*.

5.   Head through a gate and into a large field. Ahead of you, you should be able to see the sea for the first time. Pass through a second gate and then turn right along a small lane. Take the path to the right of the cottage and then continue down cycling alongside the Loe.

6.   Take the right-hand turning across the wooden causeway and turn right at the end. Take the lower right-hand path. As you get closer to the sea, the trail becomes sands until the point when it is pure sand and you will now need to get off and push.

7.   As you come onto the beach you need to turn right and head towards the

i **Penrose Estate:**
The second half of this ride travels through the more formal part of the Penrose Estate. Penrose is a National Trust estate and whilst the house itself is privately owned the rest is available to explore. There is an interesting little bath house, as well as pretty, walled gardens. These kitchen gardens are attached to the stables which now act as a great café. The house itself was the centre of a recent fascinating family history story as it was inherited

THE PENROSE ESTATE

44

house up on the cliff edge. This beach is known as the Loe Bar. You can NOT swim here. Head off the beach and up to the house. Take the cycle trail in front of the house and follow the lower route signposted *Stables Via Loe Pool*.

8.   You are now on the return journey and the route is wide, flat and well made. This side of the *Penrose Estate* is clearly signposted and easy to navigate. For these reasons, this section of the ride can be busy with a wide range of users. At the Stables, there are loos and a good café, plus a walled garden.

9.   From the Stables, take the trail across the valley and turn right at the T-junction, and cycle back to the car park. To visit the small bath house, turn left at the T-junction; you can see it in the fields on the right of the path. Having explored turn round and cycle back towards the car park.

by an unknown son, whose claim was established through a DNA test.

LINKS:

Penrose Estate
https://www.nationaltrust.org.uk/penrose
Loe Pool and Bar
https://cornishbirdblog.com/2020/08/15/
the-mystery-of-loe-pool-the-bar-helston/

PHOTO ALBUM:

https://photos.app.goo.gl/MyXVe1xfPrqFRTsF9

7

GREAT FLAT LODE – MODERATE – 8 MILES

This is an incredible route through the tin and copper mining area with lots of great views and buildings to explore. The route circumnavigates Carn Brea, which you can walk up later.

Additional Information: There are lots of junctions on this route, but it is well worth the stops and starts. It is well signposted all along the way.

This trail is extremely popular with horse riders. You are highly likely to meet a horse and will need to give way to them.

Length: 8 miles
Type: Circular
Effort: Moderate
Terrain: Hardcore and road
Off-road: 80%
Parking: King Edward Mine Museum (no purchase required but they do have a great café.) TR14 9HW
WCs: King Edward Mine Museum – Seasonal
Café/Pub: King Edward Mine Museum – Seasonal
OS Map: Explorer 104 or Landranger 203

Nearby Attractions:

- Carn Brea, an ancient hilltop site with a monument, castle and other points of interest. Stunning views in all directions.
- Gwennap Pit, a remarkable feature, off the beaten track but well worth a visit to this open-air meeting place. The pit is a deep depression in the earth, shaped into concentric rings where preachers would address their congregations.

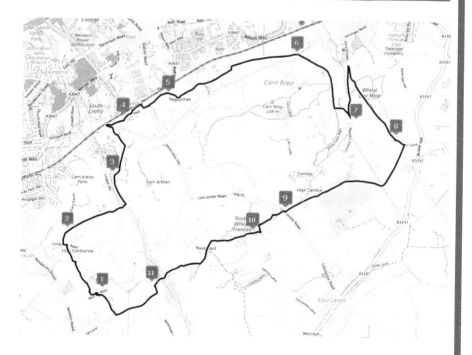

Elevation Profile

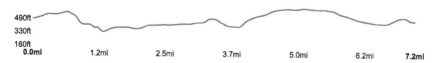

490ft						
330ft						
160ft						
0.0mi	1.2mi	2.5mi	3.7mi	5.0mi	6.2mi	7.2mi

DRAMATIC LANDSCAPES

DIRECTIONS:

1. From the car park, head onto the road, turn right and immediately take the right-hand track. Look out for the *Great Flat Lode* fingerpost. You are now cycling alongside the car park. The trail here is quite narrow. At the road junction, turn left and after a few yards turn right down another small road. Just before a property called The Bungalow, turn right and back onto the bridleway.

2. As the bridleway narrows it starts to head downhill. This section is very narrow and steep so cycle with caution. At the T-junction, cross the road and continue for a hundred metres until you get to a

Carn Brea:
Carn means a pile of rocks or a granite outcrop. As you travel around Cornwall you will see carns everywhere, but Carn Brea is one of the most dramatic as it towers over the towns of Redruth and Camborne. Carn Brea is a hilltop site that the cycle trail circumnavigates. It has been occupied since Neolithic times, with evidence dating from 3500 BC. The area

giant granite boulder for Holly Farm. Turn left before the stone and follow the trail along the left of the house.

3.   Continue through a gate and then straight across the road. After a short while, the trail opens onto a jumble of lanes and driveways and the signposts seem to disappear. Turn right, heading up towards the power lines and railway

is covered in various buildings and features, the two visible from the cycle route are the Bassett Monument and Carn Brea Castle, a hunting folly built upon the site of a former chapel.

LOTS TO EXPLORE

LOOKING UP TO CARN BRAE

bridge. Just before the bridge, turn right taking the trail beside a large metal gate. You will now be cycling with a railway line directly on your left-hand side.

4.   As the path comes down onto a road, turn left. Cycle along the road for a short section and then come off it again on the left, following the trail signpost. This path then joins another road. Turn right and cycle downhill as the road bends to the left. As the road bends sharply to the right, you need to cycle forwards heading down the No Through road. It is signposted for the Great Flat Lode and National Cycle Route 3 but this junction is a meeting point of many lanes and it's harder to describe in words than it is to see in front of you.

5.   After a few hundred yards on this lane, turn right following the signs for the Great Flat Lode. You are now also travelling along Route 3, so keep following the blue signs. We won't be on this the entire way, but it is handy for now. Cycle into a little hamlet and at the village noticeboard, turn left following the signs onto the bridleway again. Take this route for just under a mile. *Carn Brea* is clearly visible up on your right.

6. At a junction by some large rocks, you need to take the right-hand path coming off the tarmac trail. (If you find yourself cycling downhill into a small village you have overshot the turning. Head back up to the granite stones.) You are now leaving Route 3 and are following the brown mining trail sign. Continue along the unmade trail until you get to a crossroads. Take the left-hand path heading downhill.

7. As you come down onto the road, turn left and cycle downhill. Continue along the road until just before the 20-mph sign. Now turn right onto the Great Flat Lode trail. You are effectively doubling back on yourself, heading uphill on the trail.

8. At the top of the trail, cross the road and continue up Copper Lane. As the road bends to the left follow the Great Flat Lode signpost to the right, passing through a large gate. This section is popular with horse riders.

9. There are one or two gates and small lanes to cross on this section so take care. Eventually, you get to a fork in the trail. Take the right, and head through a small tunnel. At the next road junction, cross over and follow the trail until it reaches *South Wheal Frances Mine*, a large industrial site. Well worth stopping at and exploring.

Great Flat Lode:
A lode is a mining term for a mineral deposit. The minerals here were tin and copper. These lodes normally lie at an angle of sixty to ninety degrees, but this deposit ran at just ten degrees, making it easier to mine from the surface. This resulted in many mines across the deposit.

SOUTH WHEAL FRANCES MINE

10.   The trail continues just to the left of the main site with one large building to your left and the rest of the site on your right and heads downhill. Come down onto a road in front of "Thursday Cottage" and turn left. As the road bends right cycle forwards, past a row of terraced houses until the road turns into a track. As the track comes to an end, turn right along the trail towards another mine building.

11.   As you come onto a very small lane turn left. Head uphill on the lane until it bends sharply to the left, you continue forward on the trail. Again, this is nicely

i **South Wheal Frances Mine:**

This wonderfully dramatic site is a photographer's dream and a great place to have a picnic.

signposted. Shortly after you pass an engine house, there is a turning to the right. Take this and head downhill until you reach a road. You are now back where you started at the King Edward Mine Museum.

LINKS:

King Edward Mine Museum
https://www.kingedwardmine.co.uk/

PHOTO ALBUM:

https://photos.app.goo.gl/293WNL3cZT3XF76J9

8

TIN TRAIL – MODERATE – 8.5 MILES

A short but stunning ride taking in the rugged Atlantic coastline and many iconic Cornish images. The trail passes through several mining complexes and ends at Pendeen Lighthouse and a sandy beach before returning to Pendeen. It is also a good ride to spot lots of Cornish wildlife.

Additional Information: In high winds, the exposed nature of this trail can be difficult. The bridleway section is very rocky and won't suit thin bike tyres.

Length: 8.5 miles
Type: There and back
Effort: Moderate
Terrain: Road and hardcore
Off-road: 50%
Parking: Geevor Tin Mine TR19 7EW
WCs: Geevor. Botallack, National Trust
Café/Pub: Various on route
OS Map: Explorer 102 or Landranger 203

Nearby Attractions:
- Zennor, a tiny hamlet, home to a legendary mermaid and some fabulous ice cream.
- Cape Cornwall, nicknamed Little Land's End.
- St Ives, famed for its historic lanes and astounding beaches.

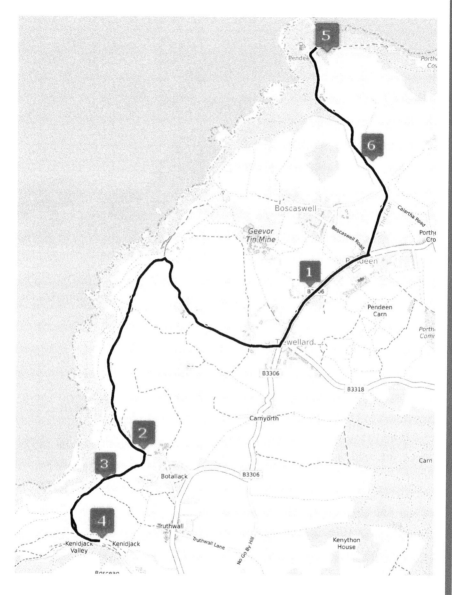

Elevation Profile

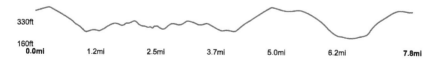

330ft

160ft
0.0mi   1.2mi   2.5mi   3.7mi   5.0mi   6.2mi   7.8mi

INDUSTRIAL ARCHAEOLOGY

DIRECTIONS:

1. From Geevor Car Park, head to the main road and turn right. Turn right just after the Trewellard Arms down to Levant. Take this road to the end, and as you approach Levant and the sea, the road becomes narrower and rougher. From the Levant Mine National Trust car park, take the bridleway on your left. You will follow this bridleway for the next mile. It is wide but rocky and will certainly give you a shake as you bump along. Keep to the bridleway at all times avoiding the smaller footpaths.

2. As you approach Botallack Mine head towards the National Trust buildings housed in the Count House. You can park your bikes here and go and explore the

Tin and Copper Mining:

This route takes in some of Cornwall's most iconic sights including the Crowns Engine House, whose mine shafts run out under the seabed. Make sure to stop at the Geevor visitor centre as well as the Botallack visitor centre to understand the surrounding landscape.

CROWNS ENGINE HOUSES

sights. Be sure to head down and visit the iconic Crowns Engine Houses.

3.   Return to your bikes and cycle along the trail until you reach the head of the Kenidjack Valley, with views over to Cape Cornwall. The tall chimney on the headland is an indication of another mine. To the left, out to sea, you may be able to spot Longships, a lighthouse on a rocky outcrop. The walk down the valley is very pretty with abandoned mining structures along the way and ends in a rocky cove. To explore you will need to push your bike rather than ride it.

4.   At the head of the Kenidjack Valley, return the way you came, passing

Wildlife:
As well as teaming with industrial archaeology, the Tin Trail is blessed with an abundance of wildlife. Including seals, basking sharks, gannets and choughs. Basking sharks are seasonal from late spring to early summer but the seals are here all year. In autumn and early winter, they become more visible as they come to shore to give birth. Never approach a seal with or without a pup. If you see a pup on its own and are concerned

PENDEEN LIGHTHOUSE

Botallack and Levant Mines and then back onto the main road (distance 2 miles). Turn left, cycling past Geevor, where you parked, and on to the village of Pendeen. As you pass the village stores you need to turn left. The road immediately branches, and you need the right-hand road sign-posted to Pendeen Lighthouse. At the next junction, turn left towards the sea. This is a scenic single-lane track that ends at the lighthouse.

5.   At the lighthouse you can follow the coast path down to the right, passing two stones with Private Property painted on them. Don't worry, this doesn't mean No Entry. The coast path is wide but rugged and you will need to walk your bikes, but Portheras Cove is a nice, sandy beach although not best for swimming due to an undertow.

call the Seal Rescue service (details in the links) but never approach it. Its mother is likely watching you from the water.

If you are lucky you might also see Cornwall's native symbol, the chough. A black bird of the crow family, it has a bright red beak and legs to match. It is an acrobat in the air and you can spend hours watching it soar and plunge as it plays on the wind. The chough had died out in Cornwall and only re-colonised in 2001 when a wild pair established themselves. Now, through careful projects to restore the numbers, choughs are back in Cornish skies and although the numbers are low they are growing. This stretch of coastline is one of the best places in Cornwall to catch a glimpse of them.

PORTHERAS COVE

6. Having enjoyed the views you now need to retrace your journey to Geevor Mine and maybe explore some of the exhibitions there and take the opportunity to go down into the tunnels.

LINKS:

Cornish Choughs
https://www.rspb.org.uk/birds-and-wildlife/wildlife-guides/bird-a-z/chough/cornish-choughs/
Cornwall Seal Group
https://www.cornwallsealgroup.co.uk/
Mining in Cornwall – St Just District
https://www.cornishmining.org.uk/areas/st-just-mining-district

PHOTO ALBUM:

https://photos.app.goo.gl/fMw9uUhYQxYMZxQW7

9

TEHIDY ESTATE AND BEYOND – MODERATE – 10 MILES

A lovely woodland ride stretching out to the Cornish cliffs. Half this ride is on small roads and whilst mostly flat there are a few big hills. For an easier and traffic-free ride, stay within the trails of the Tehidy Estate itself.

Length: 10 miles
Type: Circular
Effort: Moderate
Terrain: Road and hardcore
Off-road: 50%
Parking: Tehidy East Lodge Car Park TR16 4PS
WCs: Tehidy
Café/Pub: Tehidy. Hell's Mouth Café
OS Map: Explorer 104 or Landranger 203

Nearby Attractions:
- Portreath tidal pool.
- Heartlands, Pool. Heartlands, a nineteen-acre Cornish Mining World Heritage Site, is a family-friendly visitor attraction that embodies Cornish culture. With a mining museum and exhibition, the Diaspora Gardens, and a giant adventure playscape for kids, all completely free to enjoy.

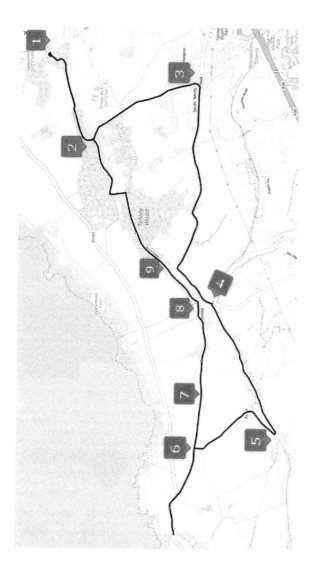

Elevation Profile

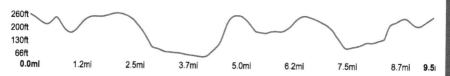

BROAD WOODLAND PATHS

DIRECTIONS:

1. From the car park follow the signs in the direction of Coombe. Cycle into the woods and away from the road. Head through the trees and then follow the path as it runs alongside a golf course. If you hear anyone shout "fore" take heed, it means a golf ball is heading in your direction at speed. The trail heads back into the trees and continue to follow the signs to Coombe.

2. At the right-hand turning for Coombe you now need to go straight ahead following the signs to the South

Tehidy and the Bassets:

The Bassets owned Tehidy from around the twelfth century only selling it in 1915. At one point they were the fourth largest landowners in Cornwall and owners of two of the most profitable mines in Cornwall. As you can imagine they were enormously wealthy. Tehidy is now run as a country

THE BEAUTIFUL CASCADES BY THE PICNIC AREA. (NO BIKES IN THIS SECTION)

Drive car park. This section has a no cycling sign so dismount just whilst you're taking this link section. As you pass through the wooden kissing gate head down the private road. Do not turn right towards *Tehidy* House. Cycle past South Drive Car Park; this is the location of the café and loos.

park by Cornwall Council and the house has been turned into private residences.

3.　Once you've passed South Lodge at the end of the road, take the right-hand slip lane and then turn right onto the main road. Follow this road for one and a half miles, until you pass a right-hand turn, signposted Hayle. Very shortly after this turning, take the public bridleway on your right.

4.　The trail is narrow and can be muddy. You can hear rather than see the Red River and after a mile, the bridleway joins a road. There is a small ford to cross, although there are some granite steps to help navigate the stream.

5.　Turn right and start to head uphill. This section gets incredibly steep and if you can make it to the top without pushing you have earned a lifetime of bragging rights. At the top follow the road as it bends around ignoring the left-hand turn and cycle up to the T-junction. There is a small diversion over to Hell's Mouth and is well worth it. See 5a.

5a.　At the junction, turn left and then as the lane joins another road turn left again. You can see the café ahead of you. Park at the café and stop for some

AN INCREDIBLE TWISTED TREE

refreshments and then head across the road and have a quick stroll along the coast path. The cliffs are extremely high here, three hundred feet, and there is virtually no protection from the edge. Proceed with care but it is incredibly dramatic. Now cycle back from the café to the T-junction where you first turned left and this time cycle on.

6.　If not visiting Hell's Mouth, turn right at the T-junction. As you cycle you can see Carn Brea in the distance. The very tall structure is the Basset Monument, which was erected by the Bassets, the owners of Tehidy. (To cycle in this area see Ride 7.) Follow the road down into Coombe.

LOOKING OUT OVER HELL'S MOUTH

7.   The turning for the bridleway is at the bottom of the hill, on your left, and easy to miss as it initially looks like a private tarmacked drive. If you reach the post box and the bridge you have overshot your turning.

8.   You are now back in the Tehidy Estate. When you get to the information board you can see that you are now travelling along West Drive and you will be making your way back to East Lodge Car Park. At the T-junction take the left-hand turning towards Kennels Hill and North Cliff Plantation. At the top of the hill turn right and cycle the final mile back to the car park.

LINKS:

Hell's Mouth
https://cornishbirdblog.com/2018/08/23/
a-potted-history-of-hells-mouth-cornwall/

PHOTO ALBUM:

https://photos.app.goo.gl/XMcGswP6zQxCWYed6

10

CLAYS TO COAST 2. ST AUSTELL/EDEN PROJECT – MODERATE – 11 MILES

This is an excellent ride passing through an alien landscape as you make your way through the china clay fields and on to the world-famous Eden Project.

Linked Ride: This is one half of the Clays to Coast route, see Ride 4.

Length: 11 miles
Type: There and back
Effort: Moderate
Terrain: Hardcore
Off-road: 95%
Parking: Priory Road Car Park, St Austell PL25 5AB
WCs: St Austell. Wheal Martyn Museum. Eden Project
Café/Pub: St Austell. Wheal Martyn Museum. Eden Project
OS Map: Explorer 107 or Landranger 200

Nearby Attractions:
- Wheal Martyn, China Clay Museum. To really understand the strange buildings and landscape around you, a trip to this museum is worth the diversion. You can visit it whilst on this cycle route.

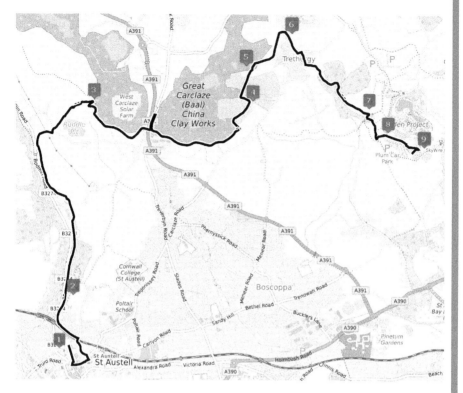

Elevation Profile

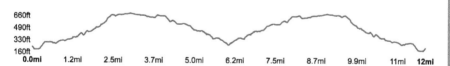

660ft										
490ft										
330ft										
160ft										

0.0mi   1.2mi   2.5mi   3.7mi   5.0mi   6.2mi   7.5mi   8.7mi   9.9mi   11mi   12mi

67

DETOUR TO MENACUDDLE WELL

DIRECTIONS:

1. In St Austell, head towards the church and then at the junction of Fore Street and Church Street, cycle up North Street. This is a steep climb. After the railway bridge, take your first left onto Tremena Road. As the road bends right, take the cycle path on the left. This section is quite narrow. The path then reaches five short wooden posts as it crosses a private lane.

(Detour – *Menacuddle Well*. As you reach the private lane, turn left and follow it down to the main road and turn right and cycle until the first small left-hand

Menacuddle Well: Menacuddle Well is located in an ornamental garden in a valley running north from St Austell. This holy well is considered to date from the late fifteenth century and is said to be one of the most beautiful holy wells in Cornwall. Traditionally the water was used for healing weak children and ulcers as well as various other illnesses.

DETOUR TO A MODERN STONE CIRCLE

turn. Cycle down to a small car park and explore the well, then return to the cycle path.)

Cross the lane and continue uphill on the cycle track. Looking to your left and right you will see ruined buildings, old remnants of the *china clay industry*. Shortly after you cycle over a bridge, there is a turning to the left, to the China Clay Museum.

(Detour – This is worth a visit and will give you a better idea of the sights ahead. It is a detour of around a mile, there and back, and clearly signposted).

Local tradition was to throw bent pins into the water for good luck.

Carry on up the path until you get to a small road. It's very quiet but what traffic there is, can be fast. Cross over and continue uphill on the cycle path. The next section is the steepest of the whole ride.

At the T-junction at the top of the path, turn right and ride until you get to the A390 flyover. As you travel along you will see *turquoise lakes* and strange *white pyramids*, all aspects of the mining industry. Cross the A390 and at the bottom of the flyover turn right. You will now be circumnavigating Great Carclaze China Clay Works, a huge opencast mine, you get the best views of the pit at the other end. Cycle on, ignoring any right turns,

China Clay Industry: For centuries China dominated the porcelain industry, exporting it to Europe where it was in high demand as the local product, fine stoneware, was considered an inferior product. In 1745, William Cookworthy was determined to locate a source of kaolin outside China and found a deposit in Cornwall. He began to refine it and triggered an industry in Cornwall, and the St Austell

THE CHINA CLAY FIELDS

until the path finally turns left, uphill. If you look to your left, you can see down into the pit.

2. Follow the path until you get to a bench on the left and a pylon on the right.

(Detour – There are two nice diversions here. On your left, you can walk up to the top of the hill, which is a spoil heap. At the top is a modern stone circle and excellent views for miles around. Alternatively, if you cycle on to the metal five-bar gate, which is always open, there is a small footpath to the right that takes you to Carn Grey, the crop of rocks to your right.)

3. Otherwise, continue along the cycle route, which now takes a sharp right and heads downhill on a broad path. The cycle trail is clearly marked with black arrows on granite rocks, or the blue Cycle Network 2 stickers and signposts. Eventually, the path ends at a small quiet road.

4. Turn right onto the road and cycle into the village of Trethurgy. At the T-junction, turn left then almost immediately right. At the bottom of the hill, the cycle path continues off-road. This is a sharp left at the bottom of the hill, and you may overshoot it.

5. The path heads downhill through trees and fields and just as the path seems to go straight on and uphill, there

area, in particular, that became a global market which has continued for two hundred and fifty years. It has shaped almost everything that you can see in this area of Cornwall.

White Pyramids:
One of the most dramatic impacts the china clay industry has had is on the skyline around St Austell. Looking around you can see lots of large pyramid structures, the largest of which is just above Carluddon. These are tips or slag heaps from the refining process. Once, they were all white, earning them the nickname of the Cornish Alps. Now only the largest remains a whiteish grey, as the others have been terraformed and re-seeded.

LOOKING OVER TO BODMIN MOOR

is a turning to the right. There are some black arrows on granite rocks, but they aren't terribly clear. This is/was the only unclear junction on the route but may have been fixed. Anyway, turn right and continue on the path.

6. As the path gets closer to Eden there are lots of junctions but the route is well signposted. Eventually, you will get to yellow signs welcoming you to the Eden Project. Follow their directions down to the bike park. There are lockers and all facilities. You can then visit the project leaving your bike and belongings in safety.

7. Take the same route home.

Turquoise Lakes: Until you see these strange green lakes it's hard to appreciate how unusual they are. Ranging from milky blues to glowing emerald, these lakes contain water rich in mica and copper mineral deposits, a residue from the washing of the clay. The water is perfectly safe, but swimming is forbidden. These are not naturally formed lakes; they are hollowed out pits meaning the sides are sheer, and they are extremely deep and very cold.

LINKS:

A Brief History of China Clay
https://www.cornwalls.co.uk/history/industrial/china_clay.htm
The Clay Trails
https://www.claytrails.co.uk/
The Eden Project
https://www.edenproject.com/
China Clay Museum
https://www.wheal-martyn.com/

PHOTO ALBUM:

https://photos.app.goo.gl/odQvQJ9ZVQkvA1bx6

11

CAMEL TRAIL 2. BODMIN/BLISLAND – CHALLENGING – 20 MILES

This epic ride starts under a canopy of trees as it follows the River Camel up to the moors. Once on the moors, the sky opens up to a little glimpse of wilderness. The route goes over an ancient clapper bridge straddling a pretty stream that makes for a perfect picnic spot. You are also likely to spot wild horses and even the occasional cattle.

Linked Ride: This is one half of the Camel Trail, see Ride 5.

Length: 20 miles
Type: There and back
Effort: Challenging
Off-road: 50%
Terrain: Road and hardcore.
Parking: Scarletts Well Car Park, Bodmin PL31 2RS
WCs: Bodmin
Café/Pub: Snail's Pace Café. The Blisland Inn
OS Map: Explorer 109 or Landranger 200

Nearby Attractions:
- Bodmin Jail rumoured to be haunted.
- Lanhydrock House (Cornwall's flagship National Trust property).

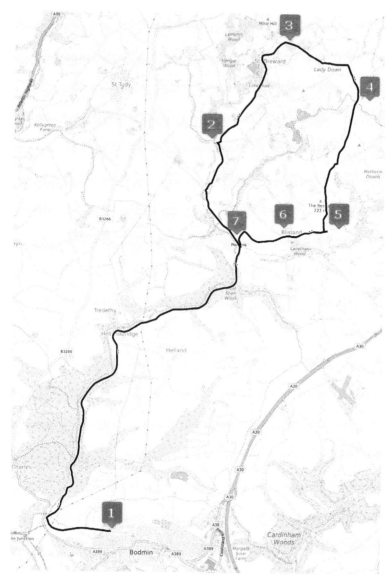

Elevation Profile

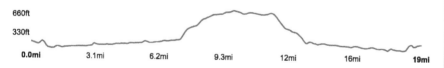

660ft						
330ft						
0.0mi	3.1mi	6.2mi	9.3mi	12mi	16mi	19mi

BODMIN AND WENFORD RAILWAY

DIRECTIONS:

1. From the car park take the clearly marked cycle trail heading away from town and onto the Camel Trail. This is the path of the old *Bodmin and Wadebridge Railway line*. After half a mile, take the right-hand turning to Wenfordbridge. Stay on this traffic-free trail for seven miles until you reach the Snail's Pace Café, ignoring any left- and right-hand turns. There are a few small road crossings; pay attention to any requests to dismount.

This is a lovely section of the trail as you cycle along a slight incline. Below to your left is the River Camel and the path is shaded by trees.

Bodmin and Wade-bridge Railway Line:
This line was opened in 1834 and closed in 1983. It was built to link the quay at Wadebridge and the quarries at Wenfordbridge, to the important trading hub at Bodmin. Minerals and sand were imported inland to try and improve the agricultural land as well as offering transportation to passengers. Despite being the first steam-powered railway line in Cornwall, it never made much

2. From the Snail's Pace Café, head onto the road and take the turning up to St Breward, this is one and a half miles and uphill all the way; I tend to get off and push. St Breward is a long ribbon village. Head through it, staying on the same road. At the end of the village just after you pass a playground on your right, take the second right-hand turning. Follow the signs for Blisland and the National Cycle Route 3 signs painted on the road.

3. After a few hundred yards, turn right at the crossroads heading towards Blisland. Once you cross the cattle grid you are up on Bodmin Moor. Sheep, cattle and wild horses are a common sight, often on the road itself. They are all perfectly

money. Passenger numbers declined and it eventually only shipped minerals. When that was no longer commercially viable the line closed.

A small section of the line still runs today, and you may be lucky enough to see a steam train arrive at Boscarne Junction that sits alongside the trail.

RIDING ALONG THE RIVER CAMEL

harmless but you might want to push your bikes past any cattle.

4.   Along this road is the beautiful clapper bridge just after East Rose, and this makes for a perfect picnic spot. Stay on this road until you reach a T-junction. Turn right and then after a short distance, take the first left-hand turning. You are still on Route 3.

5.   After the cattle grid the road starts to narrow and heads steeply downhill. At the T-junction, turn right and cycle down into the village of Blisland. Again the road is steep and narrow.

6.   Cycle through the village, keeping the village green on your left. Just after the Blisland Inn, head downhill following the road sign to Merry Meeting and

Bodmin Jail
Bodmin Jail (also still referred to as Bodmin Gaol) was built in 1779 and was one of the first built under the new reforms for more enlightened prisons. There were separate male and female wings, airy accommodation and separate cells. As well as a place of incarceration it was also a place of execution and was the site of fifty hangings. The final hanging in 1909 was of William Hampton, aged twenty-three. Hampton strangled his sixteen-year-old fiancée, Emily Tredrea following an argument; it was

PERFECT SPOT FOR A PICNIC

Wadebridge. This road is also steep and very narrow. Pay attention to any traffic and keep an eye out for passing places.

7. At the bottom of the hill the road joins another. At this junction, cross over and head across to the cycle path, just beyond the road. You have now re-joined your earlier path alongside the River Camel. Head left and cycle six miles back to the car park.

said she had wanted to call an end to their engagement. His was the last execution in Cornwall. The prison closed in 1927. Today it is a hotel and tourist attraction.

FRIENDLY LOCALS

LINKS:

Bodmin Moor
http://www.cornwall-aonb.gov.uk/bodminmoor
Bodmin Railway
https://bodminrailway.co.uk/

PHOTO ALBUM:

https://photos.app.goo.gl/yXXTVKPbpvhshVTL7

12

COAST TO COAST/ PORTREATH START – CHALLENGING – 24 MILES

The only cycle route connecting the north and south coasts. Starting at the beach resort of Portreath you cross the spine of Cornwall, passing tin and copper mines and an urban heartland that is often overlooked by tourists. The path then heads down to the Creekside village of Devoran.

Length: 24 miles
Type: There and back
Effort: Challenging
Terrain: Road and hardcore
Off-road: 70%
Parking: Portreath Car Park TR16 4NN
WCs: Several along the way attached to cafés
Café/Pub: Several along the way
OS Map: Explorer 104 or Landranger 203 & 204

Nearby Attractions:
- Tehidy Country Park. Good for woodland walks and also has a small cycle trail.
- Portreath tidal pool.
- Heartlands, Pool. Heartlands, a nineteen-acre Cornish Mining World Heritage Site, is a family-friendly visitor attraction that embodies Cornish culture. With a mining museum and exhibition, the Diaspora Gardens, and a giant adventure playscape for kids, all completely free to enjoy.

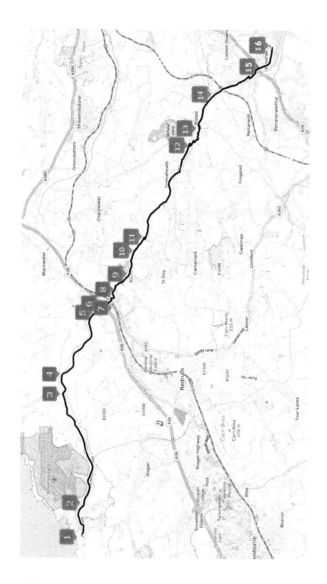

Elevation Profile

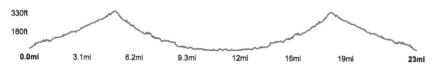

PORTREATH BEACH

DIRECTIONS:

1. From the beach car park, head out of the village taking the flat left-hand road. Just after the large metal anchor on your left-hand side, take the left-hand turning into Sunnyvale Road. This is a small residential road. As the road veers to the right heading downhill, the trail now continues ahead.

This trail is The Cornish Way and is well labelled all along the route. It often uses the engine house symbol engraved on large granite markers. The route is twelve miles and always heading towards Devoran.

Mining:
Cornwall's greatest wealth comes from the rocks beneath our feet and throughout this ride, you will see evidence of copper, tin and arsenic mining as well as other smaller deposits; lead, cadmium, uranium, gold and zinc. The one mineral still mined today is kaolin, the foundation of the modern Cornish mining industry,

2.   Go through the gate and onto the trail. This section runs for one and a half miles and crosses a few small lanes and drives. Ignore any turnings and be aware of traffic whenever you cross a road.

3.   As the trail joins a small road, head downhill to the junction. Cross the major road and join the cycle path on the other side of the road turning left. Follow the cycle path for a mile until it stops at a road junction. Turn right and head downhill. This is a quiet lane.

4.   At the next junction marked Lower Forge, cross the road and make your way along the much smaller lane directly in front of you. At the next junction, cross over and you are now back onto a public bridleway. Stay on this trail for one and a half miles.

5.   At the T-junction at the end of the trail there is a very large metal fence on the other side of the road. Turn left and immediately take the cycle path on the right-hand side of the road. This is sometimes obscured by parked cars.

6.   At the top of the trail, turn right onto the pavement and cycle past the entrance to Rodda's factory. Continue on the pavement. There are a lot of busy roads here but you will not have to join them. You are now going to cross the A30. Cyclists are asked to dismount for this section, presumably because of crosswinds and traffic hazards. Stay on the pavement and

although the mining of lithium, the basis for modern batteries, is now being investigated.

GRANITE MARKER

turn right until you are level with a traffic island. Now cross the road, and then cycle up the left-hand turning, passing the Crossroads House Care Home, and under a railway bridge.

7. After the railway bridge, the road bends to the left. Follow until you reach the pub sign for the Fox and Hounds. Now cross the road and take the small lane that runs alongside the pub car park. As it joins another road, cross at the island and cycle along the pavement.

8. At the next junction, turn right onto the cycle path and head downhill. The path will cross the road halfway down. The road is quiet but fast so take care crossing. Now continue downhill on the cycle trail.

9. After a while, the trail enters Unity Woods and you can see lots of *mining* buildings all around. Ignore all turns and continue until you reach a T-junction with a small road.

UNITY WOODS

10. Turn right onto the road and head downhill. At the next junction, cross the road and continue downhill. This is a very quiet lane. At the next T-junction by Mole End cottage, turn right and pass the sign for Poldice Valley. You are now off-road again.

11. Turn left just after the entrance sign and follow the main trail. At one point the path drops down and crosses a small stream. In summer this can just be a few wet rocks, in winter it will be more obvious. Continue bearing left and make sure you are on the higher of

> ℹ **Nature Reserves:**
> Centuries of excavation have left their toll on the landscape but a lot is being done to heal the land and bring back wildlife and people into the area. As you cycle along, it becomes harder and harder to see the stark desolation that this area must have once portrayed. Only Poldice Valley gives any clue to what it once looked like.

POLDICE VALLEY

the two paths. Follow the path until it reaches a small café and a road junction. The section through the Poldice Valley is roughly a mile and a half long. As you pass the café, cycle forwards along the road for 300 metres until you see a sign for the trail on the left-hand side.

12.   Follow this trail until it ends in the large car park for Saint Piran Café and bike hire centre. Head towards the road; it is a small but fast road so take care. Turn right, cross the little bridge and then turn immediately left back onto the trail.

13.   The trail now passes through the pretty Bissoe Valley *Nature Reserve*. Cross a small lane and continue forwards. The path splits left and right. It doesn't matter which route you take, but the right-hand path can often be waterlogged after rain.

14.   You are now in *Carnon River* Valley. Pay attention to all warning signs and do not enter any of the streams or rivers. Cross the next small road and head towards an enormous viaduct. Go under the viaduct and then cross at the next small road and continue on the trail until you pass under a road bridge.

i Carnon River:
The river flows through an area described in the nineteenth century as 'the richest square mile anywhere on earth' and is now part of the Cornish Mining World Heritage Site. The whole river length from headwaters to tidal limit sadly fails the environmental quality standards (EQS) for cadmium, nickel, arsenic, copper, zinc and iron, and so fails to achieve good status for the South West River Basin Management Plan.* Even today, decades after the last mine closed, their impacts are still felt.

15. As the cycle path joins the road, head forwards cycling down Greenbank Road. Continue down to the quay, past the Devoran village hall. As you get to the quay you will need to dismount as bikes may not be ridden beyond this point.

16. Have an explore and then head home retracing your route. If you can't quite remember it, follow the instructions on Ride 13.

LINKS:

Cornish Minerals
https://www.dakotamatrix.com/content/cornish-minerals
*Environmental Impacts
https://restorerivers.eu/wiki/index.php?title=Main_Page
Mining in Cornwall – Gwennap District
https://www.cornishmining.org.uk/areas/
Lady Basset Baths
https://acornishjourney.wordpress.com/2020/09/08/
the-basset-baths-at-portreath/

PHOTO ALBUM:

https://photos.app.goo.gl/9wrgpqPaxPsmD5rL7

13

COAST TO COAST/ DEVORAN START – CHALLENGING – 24 MILES

The only cycle route connecting the north and south coasts. Starting at the Creekside village of Devoran you cross the spine of Cornwall, passing tin and copper mines and an urban heartland that is often overlooked by tourists. The path then heads down to the beach resort of Portreath.

Length: 24 miles
Type: There and back
Effort: Challenging
Terrain: Road and hardcore
Off-road: 70%
Parking: Limited parking in Devoran. Park at the car park on the edge of the village, Truro TR3 6PF. This ride starts at the other end of the village but you can cycle down to the estuary at either the beginning or end of the ride
WCs: Several along the way attached to cafés
Café/Pub: Several along the way
OS Map: Explorer 109 or Landranger 201

Nearby Attractions:
- Truro is Cornwall's only city and has the size and charm of a bustling county town.
- Trelissick Gardens, National Trust.

- Falmouth, a large vibrant maritime town, and home to Pendennis Castle, cafés, pubs, and restaurants as well as the National Maritime Centre.
- Kennall Vale, the very pretty remains of a gunpowder factory site. Parking is an issue.
- Gwennap Pit, a large circular depression in the land used for open worship sermons and meetings, holds 1,500 people.

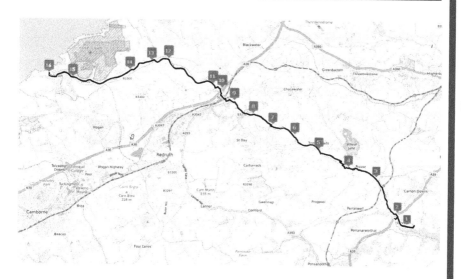

Elevation Profile

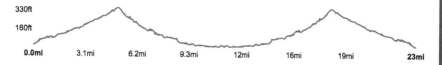

330ft
160ft

0.0mi 3.1mi 6.2mi 9.3mi 12mi 16mi 19mi 23mi

MINING HERITAGE

DIRECTIONS:

1. If you start from the car park, turn left and cycle towards the village of Devoran (away from the garage). At the T-junction, either turn right now and head toward the quay at the end of the village or do it at the end of your journey. If doing the quay later turn left onto the cycle trail. There is a fingerpost showing the image of a bike and labelled "Bridleway".

This trail is The Cornish Way and is well marked all along the route. It often uses the engine house symbol engraved on large granite markers. The route is

Mining:
Cornwall's greatest wealth comes from the rocks beneath our feet and throughout this ride, you will see evidence of copper, tin and arsenic mining as well as other smaller deposits; lead, cadmium, uranium, gold and zinc. The one mineral still mined today is kaolin, the foundation of the modern Cornish mining industry,

twelve miles and always heading towards Portreath.

2. Set off on the trail. Pass under the road bridge and into the *Carnon River* Valley. Pay attention to all warning signs and do not enter any of the streams or rivers. Ignore all left and right-hand trails and at the small road junction, cycle across in the direction of the enormous viaduct. Head under the viaduct and at the next small road junction cross over. At one point the trail forks left and right, both paths re-join each other but the left-hand fork is often waterlogged. Shortly after the two sections re-join you come to an ungated road crossing.

although the mining of lithium, the basis for modern batteries, is now being investigated.

> ℹ **Carnon River:** The river flows through an area described in the nineteenth century as 'the richest square mile anywhere on earth' and is now part of the Cornish Mining World Heritage Site. The whole river length from headwaters to tidal limit sadly fails the environmental quality standards (EQS) for

HEADING UNDER THE VIADUCT

BISSOE VALLEY

3. Cross the road and continue along the trail. You are now in the Bissoe Valley *Nature Reserve*, managed by the Cornwall Wildlife Trust.

4. At the next road junction, turn left, joining the road. This is a fast road so cross with care. Cross the small bridge and then turn immediately left into Saint Piran Café and bike hire centre. Cycle through the car park and at the far end, take the right-hand cycle path heading uphill. Continue on this trail.

5. At the next road junction, turn right and cycle for about three hundred metres until you see a café directly ahead. To the left of the café take the cycle path that runs alongside it. This is the Twelveheads Junction and is clearly marked.

cadmium, nickel, arsenic, copper, zinc and iron, and so fails to achieve good status for the South West River Basin Management Plan.* Even today, decades after the last mine closed, their impacts are still felt.

6. When the path forks, take the right-hand path towards Portreath and now head into the Poldice Valley, evidence of the *mining* industry is all around you. When the path forks, take the higher path to the left. There are lots of paths in here but stick to this main trail. At the junction where several paths appear to converge, head downhill, crossing over the small stream and now take the wide path up on the right-hand side. The stream can be no more than a few wet rocks in summer. Follow this path to the end of the valley and then turn right. The section through the Poldice Valley is roughly a mile and a half long.

> **Nature Reserves:**
> Centuries of excavation have left their toll on the landscape but a lot is being done to heal the land and bring back wildlife and people into the area. As you cycle along, it becomes harder and harder to see the stark desolation that this area must have once portrayed. Only Poldice Valley gives any clue to what it once looked like.

7. Leaving Poldice, head up a small unmade road and then turn immediately left in front of Mole End cottage. Continue along this quiet lane until you reach a crossroads. Cross the busier road and head uphill. Take the first left-hand turning, at the granite engine house marker.

8. Cycle past the buildings and into Unity Woods. There are lots of interesting paths left and right but stick to the main path heading towards Portreath. As you leave the woods, the path becomes tarmac. Head uphill, crossing a private drive and continue uphill, until you need to crossover the main road that you have been cycling alongside. This is a fast and busy road. Get off your bike and cross with care. Turn right and continue on the cycle trail until you reach the T-junction at the top of the hill.

9. At the top, turn left and cycle along the pavement that runs directly alongside the road. Get to the pedestrian crossing and cross over. Take the small lane immediately to the right of the Fox and Hounds pub sign and at the T-junction, turn left and join the road.

10. Follow this road under the train bridge and cycle down to a T-junction.

Cross the road and head up onto the pavement. This next section will take you across the A30; stay on the shared-use pavement at all times. Turn right and follow the pavement. As you reach the A30 flyover cyclists are asked to dismount. On the other side cycle forward following the pavement as it veers left. Head past the entrance for Rodda's Clotted Cream factory and then take the cycle path turning on the left.

11. At the bottom of this small hill, beside the large metal fencing, turn right onto the trail. This is a shared-use public bridleway and driveway and for the first section may have the odd car. Stay on the path until it ends at a gate leading onto a small road, this section is roughly one and a half miles long.

12. The bridleway ends at a T-junction with a road. Cross the road and now cycle along the lane. At the next crossroads, cycle forwards, passing one of the granite route markers. At the next T-junction turn left and cycle on the shared-use pavement, not the road. Pay attention as the path crosses driveways and private turnings.

13. As you pass the village sign for Cambrose, the pavement ends. Cross the road at the traffic island and head uphill on the road opposite. Within a few

DEVORAN CREEK

metres of being on this road, turn left and you are now back on The Cornish Way. Again, there is a granite marker.

14. Stick to this path until you reach Portreath, approximately one and a half miles. There will be a few minor crossings of small roads; cross each with care. In this section, there is some evidence of tramlines showing the pad stones that the rails would have rested on. At one point the trail forks. Take the smaller right-hand path and carry on. You do not want to join the main road.

15. This trail ends at a gate; head onto a small road and turn right. Follow this into the centre of Portreath and when it gets to a T-junction turn right and stay on the road until you get to the beach. There are public loos here as well as plenty of places to park your bike. The Hub is a great café and cycle hire centre sitting just above the beach.

16. Have an explore and then head home retracing your route. If you can't quite remember it, follow the instructions on Ride 12.

LINKS:

Cornish Minerals
https://www.dakotamatrix.com/content/cornish-minerals
*Environmental Impacts
https://restorerivers.eu/wiki/index.php?title=Main_Page
Mining in Cornwall – Gwennap District
https://www.cornishmining.org.uk/areas/

PHOTO ALBUM:

https://photos.app.goo.gl/9wrgpqPaxPsmD5rL7

OTHER CYCLING OPTIONS IN CORNWALL

There are many dedicated cycle parks in Cornwall with lots of epic black routes, for your death-defying gnarly riders. The following two have a range of routes aimed at all levels of riders, from those who have just removed their stabilisers to the daredevils that make me gasp in wonder as they fly past. They also have great facilities that make for a great family day out with good walking trails as well as bike routes.

Lanhydrock Bike Tracks
Set in the National Trust Lanhydrock Estate, these trails make for a great day out and can be combined with a visit to one of Cornwall's great houses. The trails sit to the south of Bodmin.

Cardinham Bike Tracks
An absolute gem of a cycling hub. Cardinham trails are based in Cardinham Woods just to the north of Bodmin.

In addition to these parks, there are a few dedicated centres for more extreme cycling.

- Woody's Bike Park nr Fowey
- Bike Park Kernow nr Grampound Road
- The Track nr Redruth

National Cycle Network Route 3
This is the main cycle route through Cornwall, with the following tributaries: 2, 32, 305, 323, 327. It runs from Land's End up to Bude on the Cornish north coast before continuing up to Bristol. The route is predominantly on small lanes although there are a few long sections on cycle trails.

The ultimate aim of the National Cycle Network is to offer a completely traffic-free network, which will be fabulous. For now, though, they make sure they travel on the quietest of roads. Just remember, in Cornwall in the summer you never know when you will encounter a lost caravan with a driver swearing at their satnav.

https://www.sustrans.org.uk/find-a-route-on-the-national-cycle-network/route-3

West Kernow Way
A new 140-mile circular bike-packing route taking in a figure of eight exploring the western end of Cornwall.

From their website:

"The West Kernow Way takes in many of the highlights of the western half of the Cornish peninsula, including the Botallack tin mines, the Bronze Age monument Mên-an-Tol, Land's End, St Michael's Mount and Lizard Point. Expect spectacular coastal scenery, hedgerows bursting with wildflowers, and ancient tracks across isolated moorland.

There's no denying it will be a challenge, with over 4,200m of climbing – but all that exertion provides a worthy excuse to sample the excellent Cornish cuisine. Designed to be ridden over three to four days, the route links together bridleways, byways, lost ways, and quiet lanes to escape the tourist hotspots and discover hidden treasures which reveal the history and culture of the region."

https://www.cyclinguk.org/west-kernow-way

EXTRA HELPINGS

ELECTRIC BIKES – YES OR NO?

I recently decided to try out an electric bike. Most hire shops have an electric option and I thought I would try them out to see what all the fuss was about. I went to the Pentewan Valley Cycle hire centre as I know the owners to be friendly and well-informed. Plus they are on the cycle route I know best, the Mevagissey to Eden route.

Andy and Rachel have two types of electric bikes and we discussed which one I should use. Given the distance I was planning on, we settled on the Raleigh. Andy ran me through all the technicalities, of which there were very few, adjusted my seat, and that was that, a very simple procedure.

Riding the bike is very easy. It's a step-through and I felt like I was back on a sit up and beg. On the right handlebar, you rotate through the seven gears. On the left handlebar, you just press either plus or minus for more or less power. Child's play. First things first, if you stop pedalling, the bike stops. This is not some sort of scooter or moped, it's more power-assisted pedals. So I was actually going to have to put some effort in, and with my illusions shattered I pushed off!

If I'm honest, I wasn't much enjoying myself. Despite having had my seat adjusted for me, I realised that I don't much like hire bikes. They're not *my* bike. That's not their fault, they just feel odd. And I wasn't sure how "odd" would translate after twenty-eight miles.

My feelings of disappointment continued. The bike was very heavy and only had seven gears. I was finding it an effort just to ride on the flat trail. At this point, the battery was switched off. The idea of having the battery on when I was on the flat was ridiculous, although in fairness the battery said it had about 101 miles in it. I wasn't worried about using up all the power; after all, the bike is still a bike even if you fully drain the battery. It just felt like cheating. I decided to drop into sixth gear and whilst it was easier on the thighs, I was having to pedal faster. So initially, I was unimpressed.

I continued and got to the bottom of the Heligan hill; for those that don't know it, this is a long and gradual hill leading up towards Heligan. The electric bike has four electric settings: Eco, Tour, Sport and Turbo. I switched to turbo and was off like a whippet. It was hilarious. I zoomed past two ladies who were so impressed with my uphill speed that I had to shout back it was electric. I didn't hear their reply as I was already too far away. In fact, halfway up I switched to fourth gear and the second electric setting as I didn't want to wear out the battery and it didn't warrant me using it to the max.

At the top of the trail the hill flattens out although there are still a few rises and falls. This was when I started to really work out how to use the bike; you need to keep in a lower gear and flick on the boost to get you over the bump, the weight of the bike is an issue otherwise. But it is an electric bike, it is designed that you use it as such, and it had taken me a while to work that out. Downhill I switched it off, and on the flat it was often off, but any rise and I clicked the power assist back on.

Now, coming back out of Mevagissey was going to be the big test. If anyone knows that hill on the cycle path you know there's a 'get off and push' bit. Well, not this time! I did the whole section. First gear and turbo. I was well chuffed. Cheating? Maybe. Thrilled to have done it? Absolutely.

I continued through St Austell and on over to Eden and there was only one aspect with which I was unhappy. This particular bike was not a mountain bike, it wasn't even a hybrid. Which meant that some of the rough sections were hard work. The weight and speed of the bike made it skittish on the loose section and the low suspension did little for my seat. The tyres are also better suited to a solid surface. There was only one section where this was an issue and if I was less happy I could have got off and pushed.

Throughout my journey, I got better and better at learning how to make the most of the bike and ultimately enjoyed the experience. I didn't need to stop once. Every hill was a doddle and I was surprised how quick it all was. Rachel and Andy were amazed to see me back so soon and even gave me a half day's refund. I also had loads of miles left on my bike.

- So to sum it up, would I like one for myself? Yes, they are great fun.

- Would I recommend it? In a heartbeat. It's brilliant and if you are someone who doesn't want to go cycling because you're worried about holding everyone else up then this is for you, it will be your turn to wait for them.

- Is it cheating? In response, I would have to ask, are gears cheating? It's not cheating at all. It's a way to offer greater access for people. It requires less effort but some people have less effort to give and this gives them the ability to get on their bike and ride. And I'm all for that.

I SPY

CELTIC CROSS

In some parts of Cornwall, you could constantly trip over these, there are so many. They come in all shapes and guises but very few are a straightforward cross shape. In the past, they were moved around a lot and were also re-used as footbridges, foundation stones or gateposts, as well as cattle rubs.

GRANITE TOR

Weather erosion has created these incredible structures on the top of some hills. These are strangely shaped boulders, perching on top of each other. Bonus points if you find one with a Logan Stone. This is a rock that rocks and pivots when you stand on it.

WIND TURBINE

Over the past few years, these giant white turbines have popped up all over the landscape.

DRIES

An industrial building used in the processing of china clay, this is an exceptionally large, long, low structure with a massive chimney at one, or both, ends. Usually, it will be hidden under years of trees and ivy, though some have been converted into flats.

ENGINE HOUSE

A tall upright building with a massive chimney on one side. Easily spotted due to their isolation and height. Engine houses are most commonly associated with tin mines; they were used to pump water out of the shafts below ground. Some of the mines even run below the seabed.

CASTLE

We have several castles in Cornwall and most of them seem to be round. As well as Mediaeval and Tudor castles we also have ancient hillforts and strongholds, including Tintagel, the suggested birthplace of King Arthur.

LIGHTHOUSE

Some of our lighthouses were built simply as automated lights, some, however, were once occupied. The Lizard Lighthouse was the last one to remain staffed and was only switched to an automated system in 1998. Many have now been turned into holiday homes.

CHOUGH

Easily distinguished by their bright red beaks and feet, and by their aerobatics, Cornwall's national bird can be found mainly on the cliffs to the west of the county. At one point they disappeared from our shores altogether and only recently has a group started to re-colonise the country to the extent that they are now starting to spread slowly but surely east.

BUZZARD

A large, brown, bird of prey, often mistaken for an eagle, but we don't have any of them. If you see crows or gulls mobbing a larger bird it will probably be a buzzard. Keep an eye out for telegraph poles as they like to perch there.

MUSSELS

One of nature's natural bounties and the easiest shell-fish to identify with their long blue-black oval cases. Archaeological records show that we have been eating mussels for the past 20,000 years.

CRAB

Alive or on the fish stand, either will do. A popular summer activity is crabbing from a harbour wall, although you will never catch a crab large enough to eat. Get a line with a hook on the end, bait it with a bit of bacon, and drop it in the water. Lo and behold, a few minutes later you'll have hooked a crab. Have a look, then throw it back in the sea.

SEAWEED

Well, what's the fun in not having an easy one to spot? Most seaweed is edible. In fact, several places in Cornwall now have it on the menu. Order some, it's really tasty.

SEAL

Like cows and dogs, seals are friendly and curious. They often come into harbours for easy food and to have a nose about. On coastal walks, they will often pop up if they hear new sounds and seem to like listening to singing.

FOXGLOVE

These lovely tall pink spires herald early summer and grow wild across Cornwall. The Cornish hedgerows are a sight to behold in spring, although you wouldn't want to bump into one as they are granite walls covered in earth and plants.

SURFBOARD

We've been surfing in Cornwall ever since St Piran arrived in Cornwall, surfing in on a millstone, from Ireland. Surfing gained mass appeal at the beginning of the twentieth century using boogie boards or belly boards. It didn't take long before people switched over to standing up on much larger boards. Bonus points if you spot an old-style wooden boogie board.

FISHING BOAT

Another easy spot but see if you can identify some of the registrations. FY means the vessel was registered in Fowey. PW is Padstow, PZ is Penzance, SC is the Scilly Isles, SS is St Ives and FH is Falmouth. Bonus points for TO, which is Truro.

CORNISH LANGUAGE

The best place to spot this is on road signs but have a look around and you'll find it in all sorts of places. The language died out in 1770 but following a concerted effort, there are now several hundred Cornish speakers, although as yet, there are no native speakers. Give it time.

PASTY

A shy beast and often misrepresented. In the past, a pasty was a worker's lunch and was filled with whatever was to hand, including fish or fruit. Today, a traditional pasty is filled with steak, taken from the skirt cut of beef, swede, potatoes, onion, salt, butter and pepper. Nothing else. It must also be crimped on the side, not over the top. The pasty has even got a protected specialist status, detailing these features.

CORNISH PLACE NAMES AND LANGUAGE

The words you see and hear in Cornwall look very different to the rest of England. This is because Cornwall once had its own language, which was in use up until the 1700s. The Cornish language is part of the Celtic family and shares a lot of similarities with Welsh and Breton. In fact, many Welsh speakers recognise a lot of Cornish place names and sayings from their language.

Cornish today is being spoken once more and although there are no native speakers yet, the language is all around you. The Cornish dialect has developed through a blend of two languages, English and Cornish, which means that things aren't always pronounced the way you may expect.

This quick little guide should help you through some of the more popular sayings, words, pronunciations, and a translation for some of the place names.

Dialect

Aw right/alright – Hello, how are you. The response is, 'aw right, you?'

Backalong – Sometime in the past.

Brock – Badger.

Cousin Jack (Jill) – This was the name given to Cornish men (and women) who went to work in the mines overseas. It is also the name given to a certain type of stone wall where the topping stones stand up like jagged teeth.

Crib – Mid-morning snack. St Austell brewery has recently resurrected the factory whistle blowing at ten every morning, signalling a crib break for the workers. The steam whistle can be heard over a great distance.

Dreckly – This means I'll get around to doing that soon. It's been likened to the Spanish *mañana* but it's not so urgent!

Furze – Gorse. The lovely bright yellow spiky bush that blooms all year round in Cornwall.

Geddon – Lots of meanings for this one depending on where you are, and the context of the sentence. Are you joking? That's incredible. Hello. Goodbye.

Heller – A child throwing a proper tantrum.

Lover – Friendly greeting. Alright, lover. Can be used with a total stranger, male or female.

Mizzle – Not quite mist or rain but certainly wet.

Ope – A small little alleyway.

Proper job – This is excellent.

Right on – I agree with you.

Some – Very. It's some hot, some wet, some busy.

Teasy – Tearful, fretful.

Up North, Away, Up Country, Foreigner – Basically, all these phrases refer to anyone or anywhere past the River Tamar.

Wasson – What's On? What's going on?

Cornish Words

The Cornish language is most visible in the placenames. There is a little rhyme that notes how much the language is still in effect in Cornwall.

By their names Tre, Pol, Pen, ye shall know the Cornishmen.

If you look at the list below you can work out what a lot of local towns and villages mean.

Bos/Bod – home or dwelling.

Carn – a pile of rocks.

Cos – a forest, a wood or group of trees.

Eglos – church.

Hayle – an estuary.

Lan – a sacred enclosure such as a church, monastery etc.

Maen (Men) – a stone.

Pen – an end of something, a headland or head.

Perran – named after St Piran/St Perran, the patron saint of tinners.

Pol – a pool.

Porth (Port) – a bay, port or harbour.

Ros – a moor, heath, or common.

Ruth – red.

Towan – sand dunes.

Tre – a homestead and its nearby buildings, literally a town.

Venton/Fenton – a spring or fountain.

Wheal – a mine.

Pronunciations

Fowey – Rhymes with boy, just one short syllable.

Mousehole – Mowzle.

Launceston – Lansun or Lawnston, at a push.

Mevagissey – Mevagissey. Yes, I know this is identical but so many people muddle it up and call it Megavissey. To be on the safe side just call it Meva.

A couple of names beg for a French pronunciation but let's keep it Cornish.

Delabole – Dellerbowl.

Doublebois – Double Boys.

Roche – Roach.

RECOMMENDED READING

Reading a story set in the place where you are staying/living, always adds an extra something. When the author describes a scene, you are instantly drawn into the book, especially when you can actually see it, not just imagine it! The following stories are all set in Cornwall and make for a great read.

Jamaica Inn – Daphne du Maurier
Historical fiction based around Bodmin Moor

Rebecca – Daphne du Maurier
Gothic romance based around Fowey

The Wind in the Willows – Kenneth Graham
Children's classic based around Fowey

Mousehole Cat – Anthonia Barber
Beautiful children's book based around Mousehole

Fault Lines – Robert Goddard
Thriller based around St Austell

A Year of Marvellous Ways – Sarah Winman
Magical, mystical, and unforgettable. Based around the Falmouth/Truro creeks

Cornish Dreams at Cockleshell Cottage – Liz Hurley
Uplifting women's fiction based around south Cornwall

The Swordfish and the Star: Life on Cornwall's most treacherous stretch of coast – Gavin Knight
Non-fiction based around Penwith

The Levelling Sea: The Story of a Cornish Haven in the Age of Sail – Philip Marsden
Non-fiction based around Falmouth

MORE BY LIZ HURLEY

To discover more of Cornwall try one of the following walking guides, with more on their way.

CORNISH WALKS SERIES

WALKING IN THE MEVAGISSEY AREA
9780993218033 | https://amzn.to/2FsEVXN

WALKING IN THE FOWEY AREA
9780993218040 | https://amzn.to/2r6bDtL

WALKING WITH DOGS BETWEEN TRURO AND FOWEY
9780993218057 | https://amzn.to/2jd83tm

TOP WALKS IN MID CORNWALL
9780993218064 | https://amzn.to/2LTxUI8

TOP WALKS IN EAST CORNWALL
9780993218088 | https://amzn.to/2XeBNZf

A HISTORY OF MEVAGISSEY

An engaging and informative history of Mevagissey.

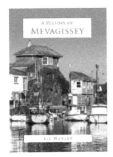

This potted history gives an insight into the history of the village and takes a humorous look behind the scenes, revealing what it is like to live and work in Cornwall's second largest fishing port. It debunks a few myths and introduces some lively, tall tales, as told through local voices.

Paperback: 978-0993218026
Digital: https://amzn.to/2r5VlkA

SCRIBBLES FROM THE EDGE

When everyday life is anything but every day.

Liz Hurley gathers her newspaper columns to deliver a collection of fast, funny reads. Join in as you share the highs and lows of a bookseller, dog lover and mother in Britain's finest county. This treasure trove of little gems moves from lifestyle pieces on living day-to-day behind the scenes in the UK's number one tourist destination to opinion pieces on education, current affairs, science, politics and even religion. Watching the sun set over a glowing beach isn't quite so much fun when you are trying to find the keys your child hid in the sand, and the tide is coming in!

Join in and discover just how hard it is to surf and look glamorous at the same time. Batten down the hatches as she lets off steam about exploding cars and rude visitors. Laugh along and agree or disagree with Liz's opinion pieces, as you discover that although life might not be greener on the other side, it's a lot of fun finding out.

Paperback: 978-0993218002
Digital: https://amzn.to/2ji2UQZ

HELLO AND THANK YOU

I hope that you've enjoyed exploring Cornwall by bike, if you have, let me know or share a review online.

Getting to know my readers is really rewarding; I get to know more about you and enjoy your feedback and photos. So it only seems fair that you get something in return. If you sign up for my newsletter you will get various **free downloads of walks** plus whatever else I am currently working on. Sometimes I am also looking for testers and beta readers. I don't send out many newsletters, and I will never share your details. If this sounds good, click on the following:

www.cornishwalks.com

I'm also on all the regular social media platforms so look me up.

#WalkinginCornwall
@WalkinginCornwall